PREFACE

1. Scope

This publication provides joint doctrine for the planning, preparation, execution, and assessment of information operations across the range of military operations.

2. Purpose

This publication has been prepared under the direction of the Chairman of the Joint Chiefs of Staff. It sets forth joint doctrine to govern the activities and performance of the Armed Forces of the United States in joint operations and provides the doctrinal basis for US military coordination with other US Government departments and agencies during operations and for US military involvement in multinational operations. It provides military guidance for the exercise of authority by combatant commanders and other joint force commanders (JFCs) and prescribes joint doctrine for operations, education, and training. It provides military guidance for use by the Armed Forces in preparing their appropriate plans. It is not the intent of this publication to restrict the authority of the JFC from organizing the force and executing the mission in a manner the JFC deems most appropriate to ensure unity of effort in the accomplishment of the overall objective.

3. Application

a. Joint doctrine established in this publication applies to the Joint Staff, commanders of combatant commands, subunified commands, joint task forces, subordinate components of these commands, and the Services.

b. The guidance in this publication is authoritative; as such, this doctrine will be followed except when, in the judgment of the commander, exceptional circumstances dictate otherwise. If conflicts arise between the contents of this publication and the contents of Service publications, this publication will take precedence unless the Chairman of the Joint Chiefs of Staff, normally in coordination with the other members of the Joint Chiefs of Staff, has provided more current and specific guidance. Commanders of forces operating as part of a multinational (alliance or coalition) military command should follow multinational doctrine and procedures ratified by the United States. For doctrine and procedures not ratified by the United States, commanders should evaluate and follow the multinational command's doctrine and procedures, where applicable and consistent with United States law, regulations, and doctrine.

For the Chairman of the Joint Chiefs of Staff:

CURTIS M. SCAPARROTTI
Lieutenant General, U.S. Army
Director, Joint Staff

Intentionally Blank

SUMMARY OF CHANGES
REVISION OF JOINT PUBLICATION 3-13
DATED 13 FEBRUARY 2006

- Identifies the *information environment* as the aggregate of individuals, organizations, and systems that collect, process, disseminate or act on information.

- Defines *information-related capabilities* (IRCs) as tools, techniques or activities employed within a dimension of the information environment, which can be used to achieve a specific end(s).

- Introduces the *information-influence relational framework* as a model illustrating the use of means and ways, through the applications of IRCs, to achieve an end(s) through influence of a *target audience* (TA).

- Defines TA as an individual or group selected for influence.

- Describes *information operations* (IO) as the integrated employment, during military operations, of IRCs in concert with other lines of operation, to influence, disrupt, corrupt, or usurp the decision making of adversaries and potential adversaries while protecting our own.

- Designates the *IO staff* as the combatant command focal point for IO and the *IO cell* as the planning element responsible for integration and synchronization of IRCs to achieve national or combatant commander objectives against adversaries or potential adversaries.

- Emphasizes IO must be integrated into all steps of the *joint operation planning process*.

- Articulates that it is vital to integrate multinational partners into joint IO planning, in order to gain agreement on an integrated and achievable IO strategy.

Intentionally Blank

TABLE OF CONTENTS

- **Provides an Overview of Information Operations (IO) and the Information Environment**

- **Describes IO and Its Relationships and Integration**

- **Addresses IO Authorities, Responsibilities, and Legal Considerations**

- **Explains Integrating Information-Related Capabilities into the Joint Operation Planning Process**

- **Covers Multinational Information Operations**

Overview

The ability to share information in near real time, anonymously and/or securely, is a capability that is both an asset and a potential vulnerability to us, our allies, and our adversaries.

The instruments of national power (diplomatic, informational, military, and economic) provide leaders in the US with the means and ways of dealing with crises around the world. Employing these means in the information environment requires the ability to securely transmit, receive, store, and process information in near real time. The nation's state and non-state adversaries are equally aware of the significance of this new technology, and will use information-related capabilities (IRCs) to gain advantages in the information environment, just as they would use more traditional military technologies to gain advantages in other operational environments. As the strategic environment continues to change, so does information operations (IO). Based on these changes, **the Secretary of Defense now characterizes IO as the integrated employment, during military operations, of IRCs in concert with other lines of operation to influence, disrupt, corrupt, or usurp the decision making of adversaries and potential adversaries while protecting our own.**

The Information Environment

The information environment is the aggregate of individuals, organizations, and systems that collect, process, disseminate, or act on information. This environment consists of three

The joint force commander's operational environment is the composite of the conditions, circumstances, and influences that affect employment of capabilities and bear on the decisions of the commander (encompassing physical areas and factors of the air, land, maritime, and space domains) as well as the information environment (which includes cyberspace).

interrelated dimensions, which continuously interact with individuals, organizations, and systems. These dimensions are known as physical, informational, and cognitive. The physical dimension is composed of command and control systems, key decision makers, and supporting infrastructure that enable individuals and organizations to create effects. The informational dimension specifies where and how information is collected, processed, stored, disseminated, and protected. The cognitive dimension encompasses the minds of those who transmit, receive, and respond to or act on information.

The Information and Influence Relational Framework and the Application of Information-Related Capabilities

IRCs are the tools, techniques, or activities that affect any of the three dimensions of the information environment. The joint force (means) employs IRCs (ways) to affect the information provided to or disseminated from the target audience (TA) in the physical and informational dimensions of the information environment to affect decision making.

Information Operations

Information Operations and the Information-Influence Relational Framework

The relational framework describes the application, integration, and synchronization of IRCs to influence, disrupt, corrupt, or usurp the decision making of TAs to create a desired effect to support achievement of an objective.

The Information Operations Staff and Information Operations Cell

Joint force commanders (JFCs) may establish an IO staff to provide command-level oversight and collaborate with all staff directorates and supporting organizations on all aspects of IO. Most combatant commands (CCMDs) include an IO staff to serve as the focal point for IO. Faced with an ongoing or emerging crisis within a geographic combatant commander's (GCC's) area of responsibility, a JFC can establish an IO cell to provide additional expertise and coordination across the staff and interagency.

Relationships and Integration

IO is not about ownership of individual capabilities but rather the use of those capabilities as force multipliers to create a desired effect. There are many military capabilities that contribute to IO and should be taken into consideration during the planning process. These include: strategic communication, joint interagency coordination group, public affairs, civil-military operations, cyberspace operations (CO), information assurance, space operations, military information support operations (MISO), intelligence, military deception, operations security, special technical operations, joint electromagnetic spectrum operations, and key leader engagement.

Authorities, Responsibilities, and Legal Considerations

Authorities

The authority to employ information-related capabilities is rooted foremost in Title 10, United States Code.

Department of Defense (DOD) and Chairman of the Joint Chiefs of Staff (CJCS) directives delegate authorities to DOD components. Among these directives, Department of Defense Directive 3600.01, *Information Operations*, is the principal IO policy document. Its joint counterpart, Chairman of the Joint Chiefs of Staff Instruction 3210.01, *Joint Information Operations Policy,* provides joint policy regarding the use of IRCs, professional qualifications for the joint IO force, as well as joint IO education and training requirements. Based upon the contents of these two documents, authority to conduct joint IO is vested in the combatant commander (CCDR), who in turn can delegate operational authority to a subordinate JFC, as appropriate.

Responsibilities

Under Secretary of Defense for Policy oversees and manages DOD-level IO programs and activities.

Under Secretary of Defense for Intelligence develops, coordinates, and oversees the implementation of DOD intelligence policy, programs, and guidance for intelligence activities supporting IO.

Joint Staff. As the Joint IO Proponent, the Deputy Director for Global Operations (J-39 DDGO) serves as the CJCS's focal point for IO and coordinates with the Joint Staff, CCMDs, and other organizations that have direct or supporting IO responsibilities.

Joint Information Operations Warfare Center (JIOWC) is a CJCS controlled activity reporting to the operations directorate of a joint staff via J-39 DDGO. The JIOWC supports the Joint Staff by ensuring operational integration of IRCs in support of IO, improving DOD's ability to meet CCMD IRC requirements, as well as developing and refining IRCs for use in support of IO across DOD.

Combatant Commands. The Unified Command Plan provides guidance to CCDRs, assigning them missions and force structure, as well as geographic or functional areas of responsibility. In addition to these responsibilities, the Commander, United States Special Operations Command, is also responsible for integrating and coordinating MISO. This responsibility is focused on enhancing interoperability and providing other CCDRs with MISO planning and execution capabilities. In similar fashion, the Commander, United States Strategic Command is responsible for advocating on behalf of the IRCs of electronic warfare and CO.

Service component command responsibilities include recommending to the JFC the proper employment of the Service component IRCs in support of joint IO.

Like Service component commands, **functional component commands** have authority over forces or in the case of IO, IRCs, as delegated by the establishing authority (normally a CCDR or JFC).

Legal Considerations

IO planners deal with legal considerations of an extremely diverse and complex nature. For this reason, joint IO planners should consult their staff judge advocate or legal advisor for expert advice.

Integrating Information-Related Capabilities into the Joint Operation Planning Process

Information Operations Planning

The IO cell chief is responsible to the JFC for integrating IRCs into the joint operation planning process (JOPP). Thus, the IO staff is responsible for coordinating and synchronizing IRCs to accomplish the JFC's objectives. The IO cell chief ensures joint IO planners adequately represent the IO cell within the joint planning group and other JFC planning processes. Doing so will help ensure that IRCs are integrated with all planning efforts. As part of JOPP, designation of release and execution authorities for IRCs is required. Normally, the JFC is designated in the execution order as the execution authority. Given the fact that IRC effects are often required across multiple operational phases, each capability requires separate and distinct authorities.

Information Operations Phasing and Synchronization

Through its contributions to the GCC's theater campaign plan, it is clear that joint IO is expected to play a major role in all phases of joint operations. This means that the GCC's IO staff and IO cell must account for logical transitions from phase to phase, as joint IO moves from the main effort to a supporting effort.

Multinational Information Operations

Other Nations and Information Operations

Multinational partners recognize a variety of information concepts and possess sophisticated doctrine, procedures, and capabilities. Given these potentially diverse perspectives regarding IO, it is essential for the multinational force commander (MNFC) to resolve potential conflicts as soon as possible. It is vital to integrate multinational partners into IO planning as early as possible to gain agreement on an integrated and achievable IO strategy.

Multinational Organization for Information Operations Planning

When the JFC is also the MNFC, the joint force staff should be augmented by planners and subject matter experts from the multinational force (MNF). MNF IO planners and IRC specialists should be trained on US and MNF doctrine, requirements, resources, and how the MNF is structured to integrate IRCs. IO planners should seek to accommodate the requirements of each multinational partner, within given constraints, with the goal of using all the available expertise and capabilities of the MNF.

Multinational Policy Coordination

The Joint Staff coordinates US positions on IO matters delegated to them as a matter of law or policy, and discusses them bilaterally, or in multinational organizations, to achieve interoperability and compatibility in fulfilling common requirements. Direct discussions regarding multinational IO planning in specific theaters are the responsibility of the GCC.

CONCLUSION

This publication provides joint doctrine for the planning, preparation, execution, and assessment of information operations across the range of military operations.

CHAPTER I
OVERVIEW

"The most hateful human misfortune is for a wise man to have no influence."

Greek Historian Herodotus, 484-425 BC

1. Introduction

a. The growth of communication networks has decreased the number of isolated populations in the world. The emergence of advanced wired and wireless information technology facilitates global communication by corporations, violent extremist organizations, and individuals. The ability to share information in near real time, anonymously and/or securely, is a capability that is both an asset and a potential vulnerability to us, our allies, and our adversaries. Information is a powerful tool to influence, disrupt, corrupt, or usurp an adversary's ability to make and share decisions.

b. The instruments of national power (diplomatic, informational, military, and economic) provide leaders in the United States with the means and ways of dealing with crises around the world. Employing these means in the information environment requires the ability to securely transmit, receive, store, and process information in near real time. The nation's state and non-state adversaries are equally aware of the significance of this new technology, and will use information-related capabilities (IRCs) to gain advantages in the information environment, just as they would use more traditional military technologies to gain advantages in other operational environments. These realities have transformed the information environment into a battlefield, which poses both a threat to the Department of Defense (DOD), combatant commands (CCMDs), and Service components and serves as a force multiplier when leveraged effectively.

c. As the strategic environment continues to change, so does IO. Based on these changes, the Secretary of Defense now characterizes IO as the integrated employment, during military operations, of IRCs in concert with other lines of operation to influence, disrupt, corrupt, or usurp the decision making of adversaries and potential adversaries while protecting our own. This revised characterization has led to a reassessment of how essential the information environment can be and how IRCs can be effectively integrated into joint operations to create effects and operationally exploitable conditions necessary for achieving the joint force commander's (JFC's) objectives.

2. The Information Environment

The information environment is the aggregate of individuals, organizations, and systems that collect, process, disseminate, or act on information. This environment consists of three interrelated dimensions which continuously interact with individuals, organizations, and systems. These dimensions are the physical, informational, and cognitive (see Figure I-1). The JFC's operational environment is the composite of the conditions, circumstances, and influences that affect employment of capabilities and bear on the decisions of the commander

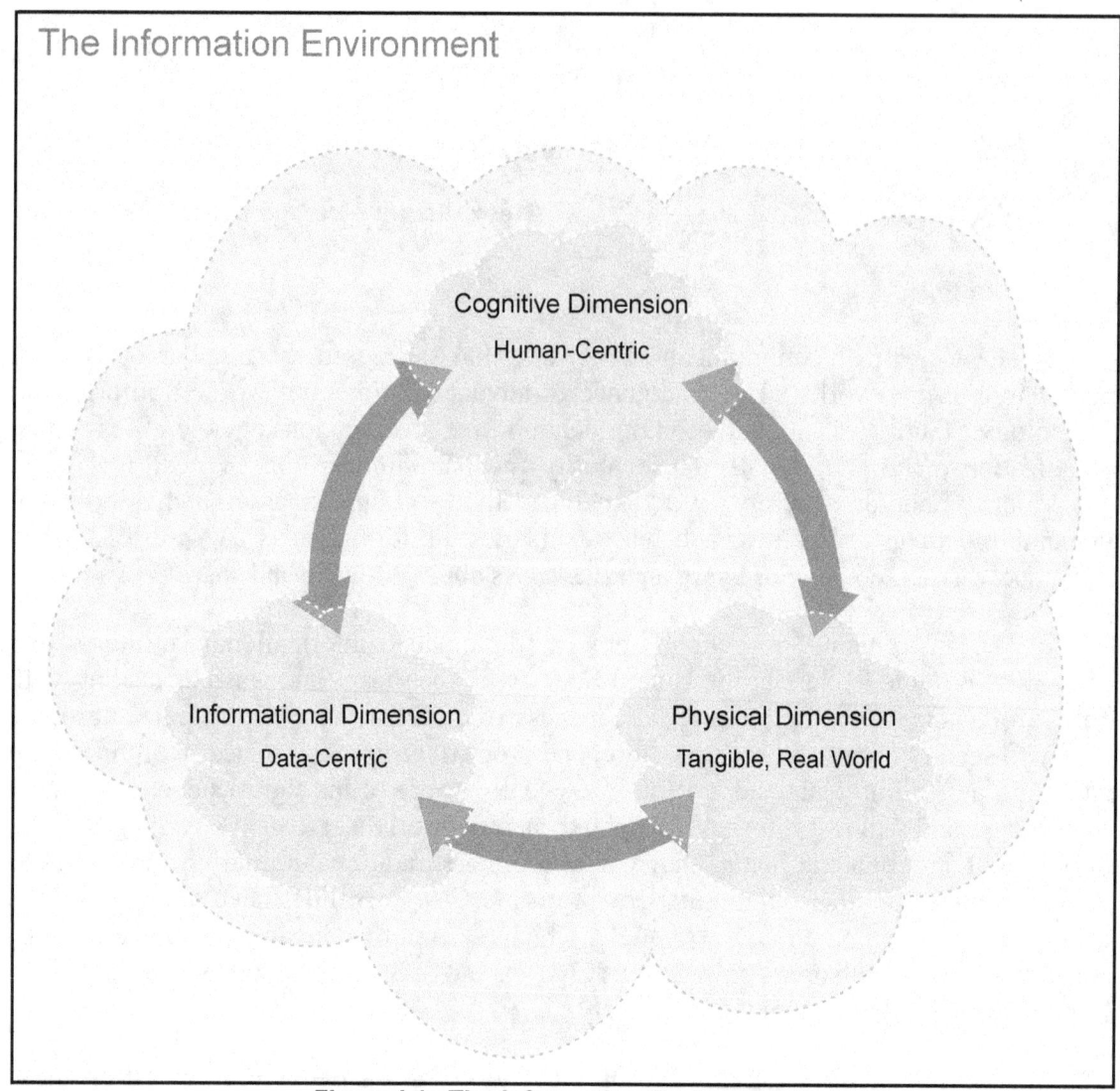

Figure I-1. The Information Environment

(encompassing physical areas and factors of the air, land, maritime, and space domains) as well as the information environment (which includes cyberspace).

a. **The Physical Dimension.** The physical dimension is composed of command and control (C2) systems, key decision makers, and supporting infrastructure that enable individuals and organizations to create effects. It is the dimension where physical platforms and the communications networks that connect them reside. The physical dimension includes, but is not limited to, human beings, C2 facilities, newspapers, books, microwave towers, computer processing units, laptops, smart phones, tablet computers, or any other objects that are subject to empirical measurement. The physical dimension is not confined solely to military or even nation-based systems and processes; it is a defused network connected across national, economic, and geographical boundaries.

b. **The Informational Dimension.** The informational dimension encompasses where and how information is collected, processed, stored, disseminated, and protected. It is the dimension where the C2 of military forces is exercised and where the commander's intent is conveyed. Actions in this dimension affect the content and flow of information.

c. **The Cognitive Dimension.** The cognitive dimension encompasses the minds of those who transmit, receive, and respond to or act on information. It refers to individuals' or groups' information processing, perception, judgment, and decision making. These elements are influenced by many factors, to include individual and cultural beliefs, norms, vulnerabilities, motivations, emotions, experiences, morals, education, mental health, identities, and ideologies. Defining these influencing factors in a given environment is critical for understanding how to best influence the mind of the decision maker and create the desired effects. As such, this dimension constitutes the most important component of the information environment.

3. **The Information and Influence Relational Framework and the Application of Information-Related Capabilities**

a. IRCs are the tools, techniques, or activities that affect any of the three dimensions of the information environment. They affect the ability of the target audience (TA) to collect, process, or disseminate information before and after decisions are made. The TA is the individual or group selected for influence. The joint force (means) employs IRCs (ways) to affect the information provided to or disseminated from the TA in the physical and informational dimensions of the information environment to affect decision making (see Figure I-2). The change in the TA conditions, capabilities, situational awareness, and in some cases, the inability to make and share timely and informed decisions, contributes to the desired end state. Actions or inactions in the physical dimension can be assessed for future operations. The employment of IRCs is complemented by a set of capabilities such as operations security (OPSEC), information assurance (IA), counterdeception, physical security, electronic warfare (EW) support, and electronic protection. These capabilities are critical to enabling and protecting the JFC's C2 of forces. Key components in this process are:

(1) **Information.** Data in context to inform or provide meaning for action.

(2) **Data.** Interpreted signals that can reduce uncertainty or equivocality.

(3) **Knowledge.** Information in context to enable direct action. Knowledge can be further broken down into the following:

(a) **Explicit Knowledge.** Knowledge that has been articulated through words, diagrams, formulas, computer programs, and like means.

(b) **Tacit Knowledge.** Knowledge that cannot be or has not been articulated through words, diagrams, formulas, computer programs, and like means.

(4) **Influence.** The act or power to produce a desired outcome or end on a TA.

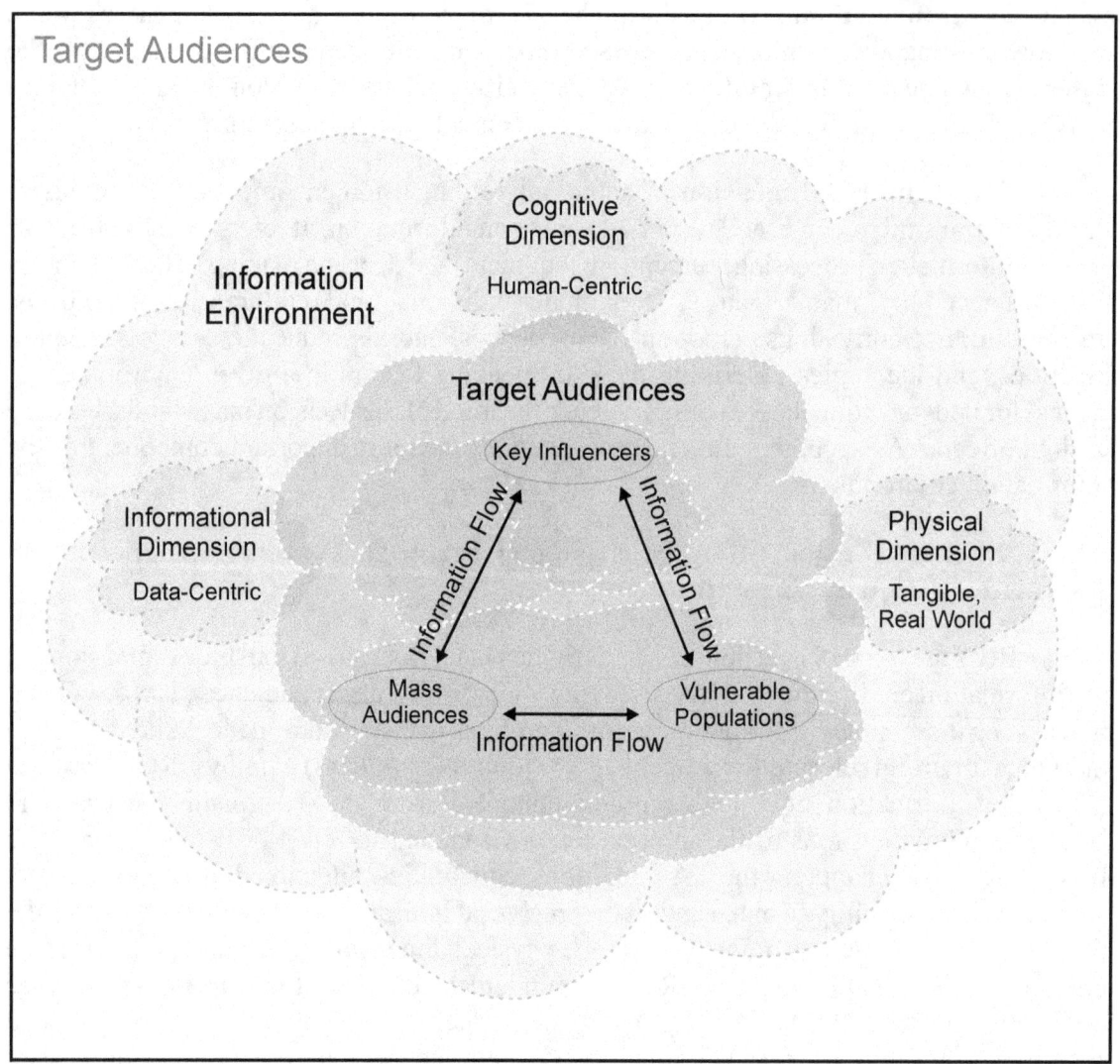

Figure I-2. Target Audiences

(5) **Means.** The resources available to a national government, non-nation actor, or adversary in pursuit of its end(s). These resources include, but are not limited to, public- and private-sector enterprise assets or entities.

(6) **Ways.** How means can be applied, in order to achieve a desired end(s). They can be characterized as persuasive or coercive.

(7) **Information-Related Capabilities.** Tools, techniques, or activities using data, information, or knowledge to create effects and operationally desirable conditions within the physical, informational, and cognitive dimensions of the information environment.

(8) **Target Audience.** An individual or group selected for influence.

(9) **Ends.** A consequence of the way of applying IRCs.

(10) Using the framework, the physical, informational, and cognitive dimensions of the information environment provide access points for influencing TAs (see Figure I-2).

b. The purpose of integrating the employment of IRCs is to influence a TA. While the behavior of individuals and groups, as human social entities, are principally governed by rules, norms, and beliefs, the behaviors of systems principally reside within the physical and informational dimensions and are governed only by rules. Under this construct, rules, norms, and beliefs are:

(1) **Rules.** Explicit regulative processes such as policies, laws, inspection routines, or incentives. Rules function as a coercive regulator of behavior and are dependent upon the imposing entity's ability to enforce them.

(2) **Norms.** Regulative mechanisms accepted by the social collective. Norms are enforced by normative mechanisms within the organization and are not strictly dependent upon law or regulation.

(3) **Beliefs.** The collective perception of fundamental truths governing behavior. The adherence to accepted and shared beliefs by members of a social system will likely persist and be difficult to change over time. Strong beliefs about determinant factors (i.e., security, survival, or honor) are likely to cause a social entity or group to accept rules and norms.

c. The first step in achieving an end(s) through use of the information-influence relational framework is to identify the TA. Once the TA has been identified, it will be necessary to develop an understanding of how that TA perceives its environment, to include analysis of TA rules, norms, and beliefs. Once this analysis is complete, the application of means available to achieve the desired end(s) must be evaluated (see Figure I-3). Such means may include (but are not limited to) diplomatic, informational, military, or economic actions, as well as academic, commercial, religious, or ethnic pronouncements. When the specific means or combinations of means are determined, the next step is to identify the specific ways to create a desired effect.

d. Influencing the behavior of TAs requires producing effects in ways that modify rules, norms, or beliefs. Effects can be created by means (e.g., governmental, academic, cultural, and private enterprise) using specific ways (i.e., IRCs) to affect how the TAs collect, process, perceive, disseminate, and act (or do not act) on information (see Figure I-4).

e. Upon deciding to persuade or coerce a TA, the commander must then determine what IRCs it can apply to individuals, organizations, or systems in order to produce a desired effect(s) (see Figure I-5). As stated, IRCs can be capabilities, techniques, or activities, but they do not necessarily have to be technology-based. Additionally, it is important to focus on the fact that IRCs may come from a wide variety of sources. **Therefore, in IO, it is not the ownership of the capabilities and techniques that is important, but rather their integrated application in order to achieve a JFC's end state.**

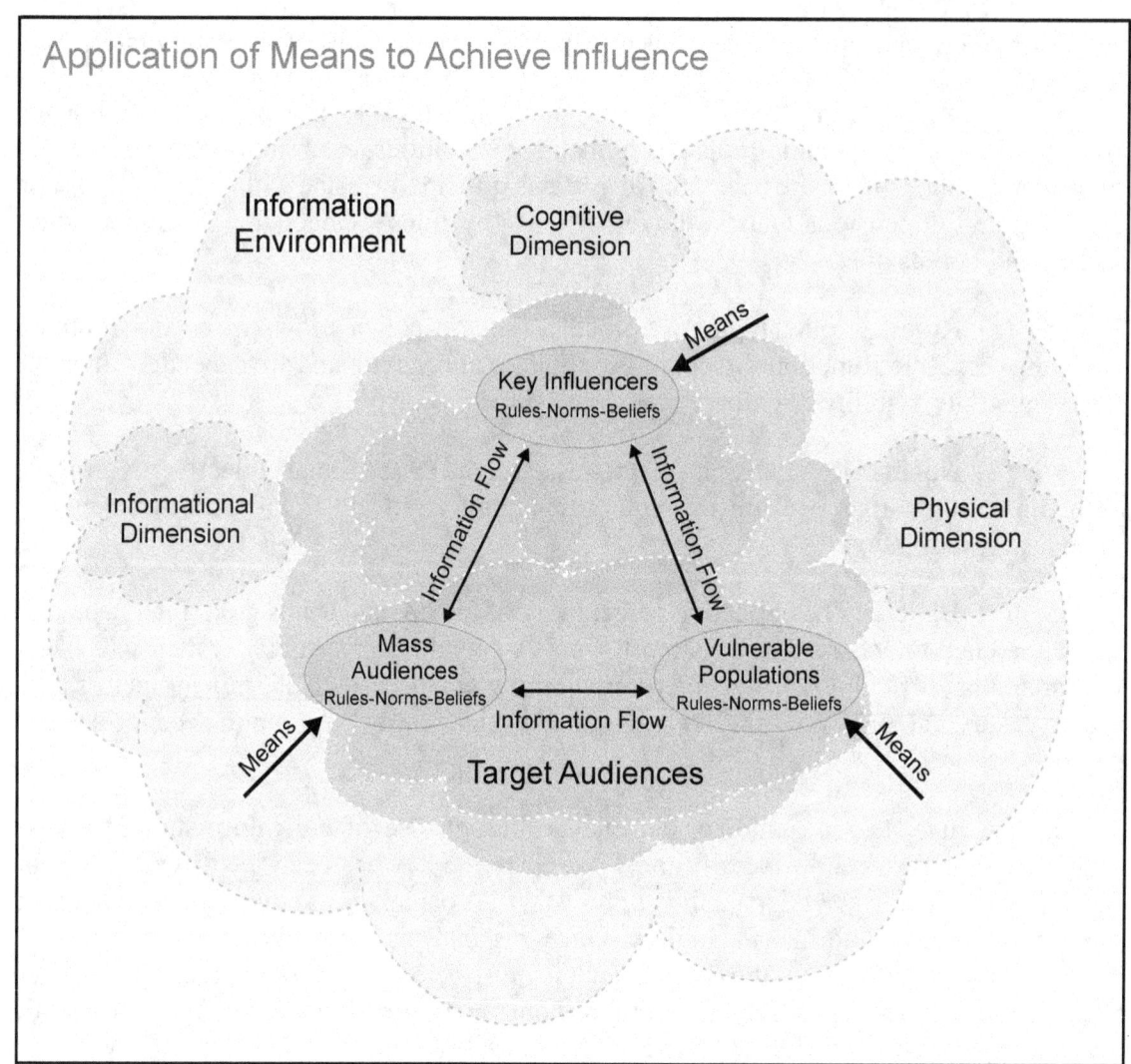

Figure I-3. Application of Means to Achieve Influence

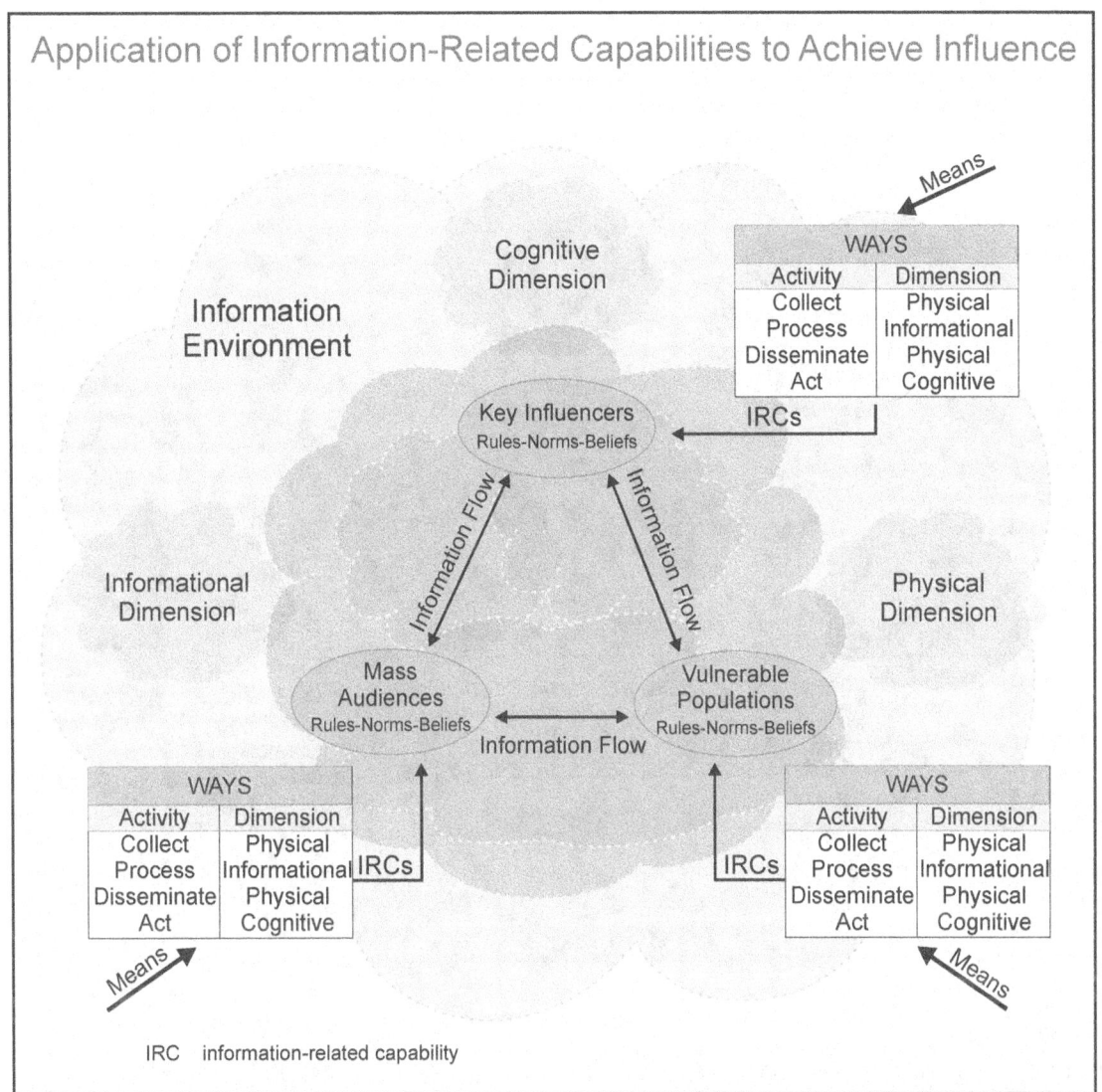

Figure I-4. Application of Information-Related Capabilities to Achieve Influence

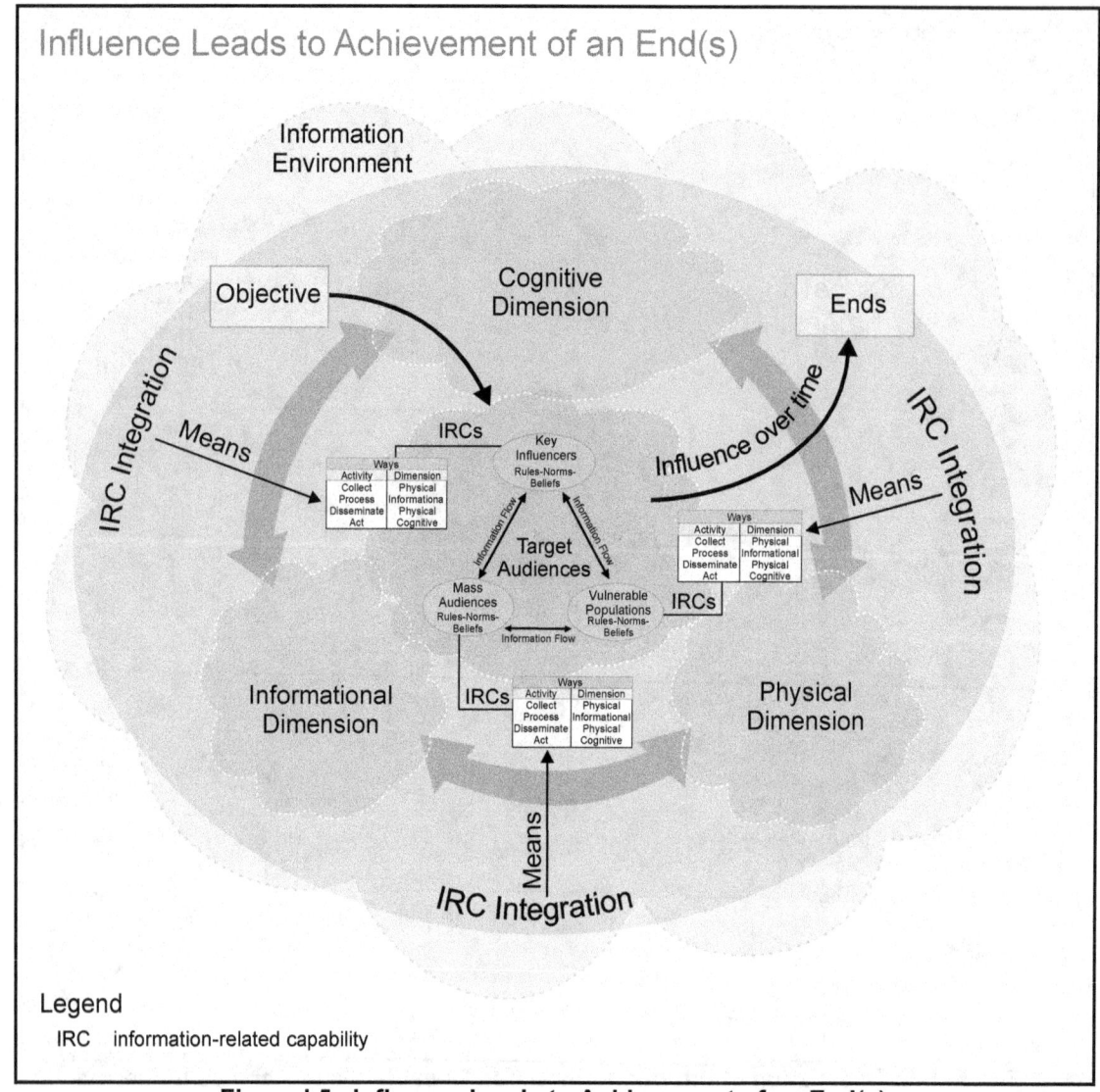

Figure I-5. Influence Leads to Achievement of an End(s)

CHAPTER II
INFORMATION OPERATIONS

"There is a war out there, old friend- a World War. And it's not about whose got the most bullets; it's about who controls the information."

Cosmo, in the 1992 Film "Sneakers"

1. Introduction

This chapter addresses how the integrating and coordinating functions of IO help achieve a JFC's objectives. Through the integrated application of IRCs, the relationships that exist between IO and the various IRCs should be understood in order to achieve an objective.

2. Terminology

a. Because IO takes place in all phases of military operations, in concert with other lines of operation and lines of effort, some clarification of the terms and their relationship to IO is in order.

(1) **Military Operations.** The US military participates in a wide range of military operations, as illustrated in Figure II-1. Phase 0 (Shape) and phase I (Deter) may include defense support of civil authorities, peace operations, noncombatant evacuation, foreign humanitarian assistance, and nation-building assistance, which fall outside the realm of major combat operations represented by phases II through V.

(2) **Lines of Operation and Lines of Effort.** IO should support multiple lines of operation and at times may be the supported line of operation. IO may also support numerous lines of effort when positional references to an enemy or adversary have little relevance, such as in counterinsurgency or stability operations.

b. IO integrates IRCs (ways) with other lines of operation and lines of effort (means) to create a desired effect on an adversary or potential adversary to achieve an objective (ends).

3. Information Operations and the Information-Influence Relational Framework

Influence is at the heart of diplomacy and military operations, with integration of IRCs providing a powerful means for influence. The relational framework describes the application, integration, and synchronization of IRCs to influence, disrupt, corrupt, or usurp the decision making of TAs to create a desired effect to support achievement of an objective. Using this description, the following example illustrates how IRCs can be employed to create a specific effect against an adversary or potential adversary.

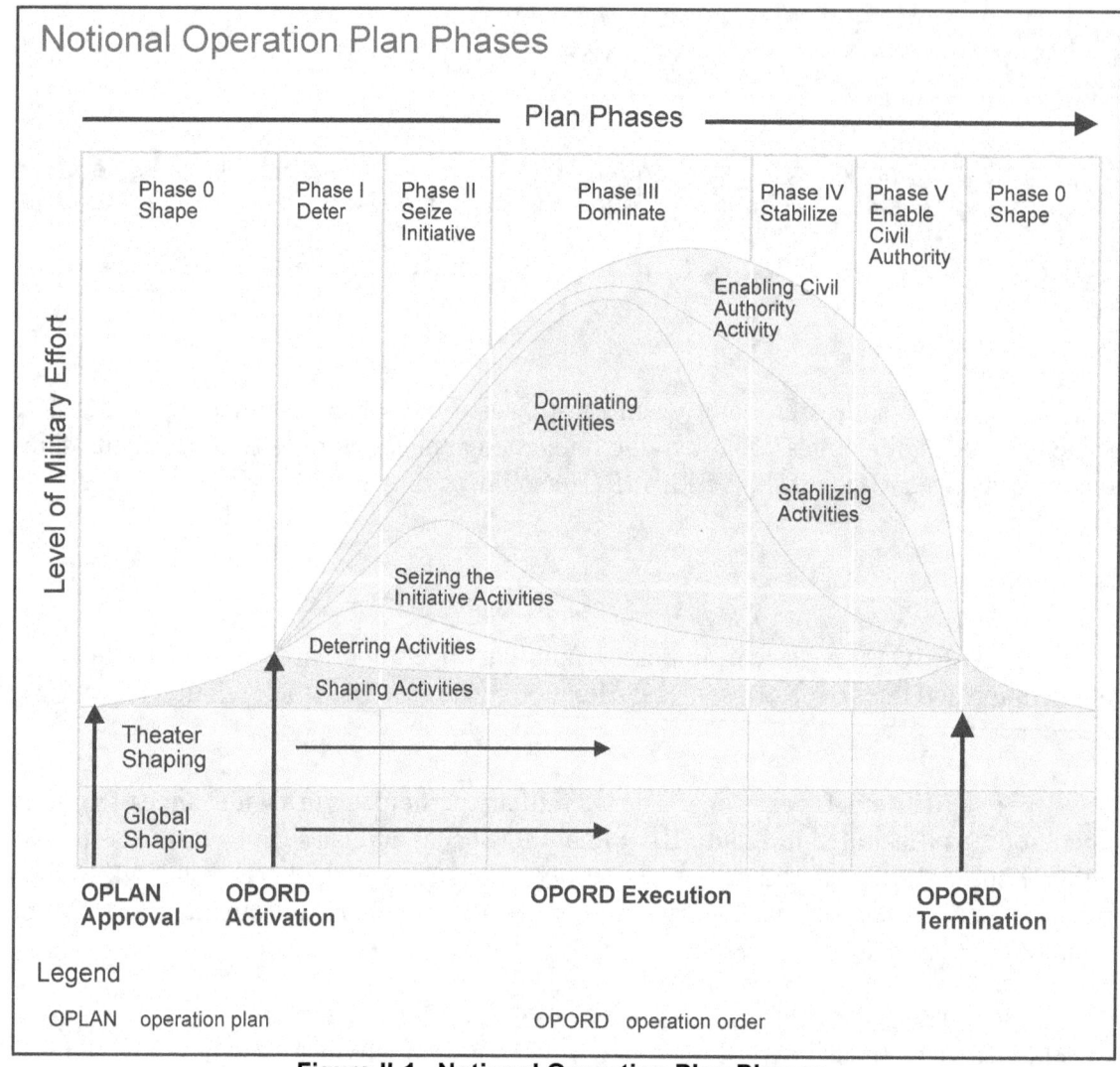

Figure II-1. Notional Operation Plan Phases

4. The Information Operations Staff and Information Operations Cell

Within the joint community, the integration of IRCs to achieve the commander's objectives is managed through an IO staff or IO cell. JFCs may establish an IO staff to provide command-level oversight and collaborate with all staff directorates and supporting organizations on all aspects of IO. Most CCMDs include an IO staff to serve as the focal point for IO. Faced with an ongoing or emerging crisis within a geographic combatant commander's (GCC's) area of responsibility (AOR), a JFC can establish an IO cell to provide additional expertise and coordination across the staff and interagency.

APPLICATION OF INFORMATION-RELATED CAPABILITIES TO THE INFORMATION AND INFLUENCE RELATIONAL FRAMEWORK

This example provides insight as to how information-related capabilities (IRCs) can be used to create lethal and nonlethal effects to support achievement of the objectives to reach the desired end state. The integration and synchronization of these IRCs require participation from not just information operations planners, but also organizations across multiple lines of operation and lines of effort. They may also include input from or coordination with national ministries, provincial governments, local authorities, and cultural and religious leaders to create the desired effect.

Situation: An adversary is attempting to overthrow the government of Country X using both lethal and nonlethal means to demonstrate to the citizens that the government is not fit to support and protect its people.

Joint Force Commander's Objective: Protect government of Country X from being overthrown.

Desired Effects:

1. Citizens have confidence in ability of government to support and protect its people.

2. Adversary is unable to overthrow government of Country X.

Potential Target Audience(s):

1. Adversary leadership (adversary).

2. Country X indigenous population (friendly, neutral, and potential adversary).

Potential Means available to achieve the commander's objective:

- Diplomatic action (e.g., demarche, public diplomacy)

- Informational assets (e.g., strategic communication, media)

- Military forces (e.g., security force assistance, combat operations, military information support operations, public affairs, military deception)

- Economic resources (e.g., sanctions against the adversary, infusion of capital to Country X for nation building)

- Commercial, cultural, or other private enterprise assets

Potential <u>Ways</u> (persuasive communications or coercive force):

- **Targeted radio and television broadcasts**

- **Blockaded adversary ports**

- **Government/commercially operated Web sites**

- **Key leadership engagement**

Regardless of the means and ways employed by the players within the information environment, the reality is that the strategic advantage rests with whoever applies their means and ways most efficiently.

a. IO Staff

(1) In order to provide planning support, the IO staff includes IO planners and a complement of IRCs specialists to facilitate seamless integration of IRCs to support the JFC's concept of operations (CONOPS).

(2) IRC specialists can include, but are not limited to, personnel from the EW, cyberspace operations (CO), military information support operations (MISO), civil-military operations (CMO), military deception (MILDEC), intelligence, and public affairs (PA) communities. They provide valuable linkage between the planners within an IO staff and those communities that provide IRCs to facilitate seamless integration with the JFC's objectives.

b. IO Cell

(1) The IO cell integrates and synchronizes IRCs, to achieve national or combatant commander (CCDR) level objectives. Normally, the chief of the CCMD's IO staff will serve as the IO cell chief; however, at the joint task force level, someone else may serve as the IO cell chief. Some of the functions of the IO cell chief are listed in Figure II-2.

(2) The IO cell comprises representatives from a wide variety of organizations to coordinate and integrate additional activities in support of a JFC. When considering the notional example in Figure II-3, note that the specific makeup of an IO cell depends on the situation. It may include representatives from organizations outside DOD, even allied or multinational partners.

Information Operations Cell Chief Functions

- Coordinate the overall information operations (IO) portion of the plan for the joint force commander (JFC).

- Coordinate IO issues within the joint force staff and with counterpart IO planners on the component staffs and supporting organizations.

- Coordinate employment of information-related capabilities and activities to support the JFC concept of operations.

- Recommend IO priorities to accomplish planned objectives.

- Determine the availability of information-related capability resources to carry out IO plans.

- Request planning support from organizations that plan and execute information-related capabilities.

- Serve as the primary "advocate" throughout the target nomination and review process for targets that, if engaged, will create a desired effect within the information environment.

- Coordinate the planning and execution of information-related capabilities among joint organizations (including components) and agencies that support IO objectives.

- Identify and coordinate intelligence and assessment requirements that support IO planning and associated activities.

- Coordinate support with the Joint Information Operations Warfare Center, Joint Warfare Analysis Center, and other joint centers and agencies.

Figure II-2. Information Operations Cell Chief Functions

5. Relationships and Integration

a. IO is not about ownership of individual capabilities but rather the use of those capabilities as force multipliers to create a desired effect. There are many military capabilities that contribute to IO and should be taken into consideration during the planning process.

(1) Strategic Communication

(a) The SC process consists of focused United States Government (USG) efforts to create, strengthen, or preserve conditions favorable for the advancement of national interests, policies, and objectives by understanding and engaging key audiences through the use of coordinated programs, plans, themes, messages, and products synchronized with the actions of all instruments of national power. SC is a whole-of-government approach, driven by interagency processes and integration that are focused upon effectively communicating national strategy.

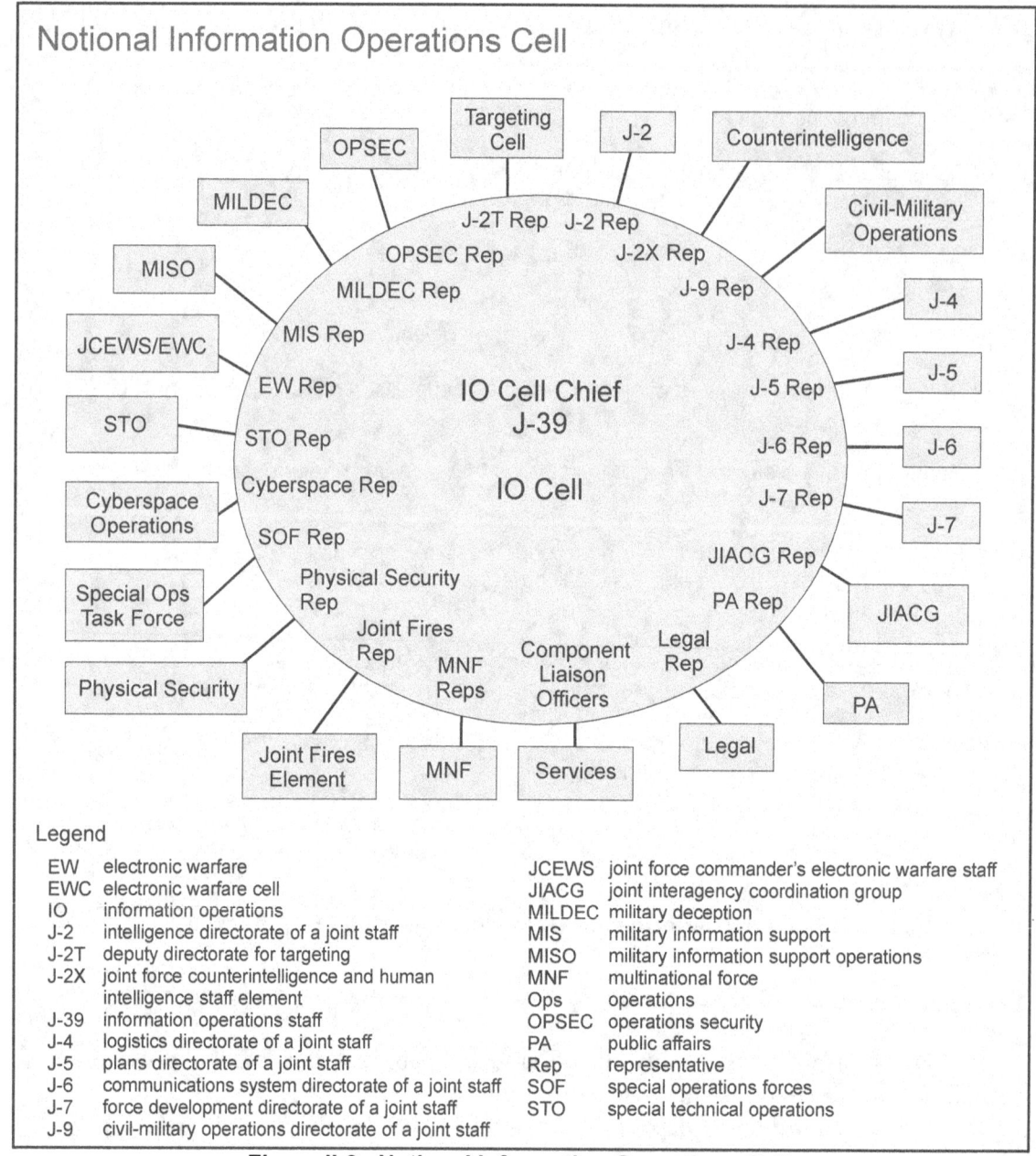

Figure II-3. Notional Information Operations Cell

(b) The elements and organizations that implement strategic guidance, both internal and external to the joint force, must not only understand and be aware of the joint force's IO objectives; they must also work closely with members of the interagency community, in order to ensure full coordination and synchronization of USG efforts. Hence, the JFC's IO objectives should complement the overall objectives in accordance with strategic guidance. The joint interagency coordination group (JIACG) representative within the IO cell facilitates coordination to comply with strategic guidance and facilitate SC.

(2) **Joint Interagency Coordination Group.** Interagency coordination occurs between DOD and other USG departments and agencies, as well as with private-sector entities, nongovernmental organizations, and critical infrastructure activities, for the purpose of accomplishing national objectives. Many of these objectives require the combined and coordinated use of the diplomatic, informational, military, and economic instruments of national power. Due to their forward presence, the CCMDs are well situated to coordinate activities with elements of the USG, regional organizations, foreign forces, and host nations. In order to accomplish this function, the GCCs have established JIACGs as part of their normal staff structures (see Figure II-4). The JIACG is well suited to help the IO cell with interagency coordination. Although IO is not the primary function of the JIACG, the group's linkage to the IO cell and the rest of the interagency is an important enabler for synchronization of guidance and IO.

(3) **Public Affairs**

(a) PA comprises public information, command information, and public engagement activities directed toward both the internal and external publics with interest in DOD. External publics include allies, neutrals, adversaries, and potential adversaries. When addressing external publics, opportunities for overlap exist between PA and IO.

(b) By maintaining situational awareness between IO and PA the potential for information conflict can be minimized. The IO cell provides an excellent place to coordinate IO and PA activities that may affect the adversary or potential adversary. Because there will be situations, such as counterpropaganda, in which the TA for both IO and PA converge, close cooperation and deconfliction are extremely important. Such coordination and deconfliction efforts can begin in the IO cell. However, since it involves more than just IO equities, final coordination should occur within the joint planning group (JPG).

(c) While the IO cell can help synchronize and deconflict specific IO-related and PA objectives, when implementing strategic guidance that affects the adversary, care must be taken to carefully follow all legal and policy constraints in conducting the different activities. For example, see Department of Defense Directive (DODD) S-3321.1, *Overt Psychological Operations Conducted by the Military Services in Peacetime and in Contingencies Short of Declared War.*

(4) **Civil-Military Operations**

(a) CMO is another area that can directly affect and be affected by IO. CMO activities establish, maintain, influence, or exploit relations between military forces, governmental and nongovernmental civilian organizations and authorities, and the civilian populace in a friendly, neutral, or hostile operational area in order to achieve US objectives. These activities may occur prior to, during, or subsequent to other military operations. In CMO, personnel perform functions normally provided by the local, regional, or national government, placing them into direct contact with civilian populations. This level of interaction results in CMO having a significant effect on the perceptions of the local populace. Since this populace may include potential adversaries, their perceptions are of great interest to the IO community. For this reason, CMO representation in the IO cell can

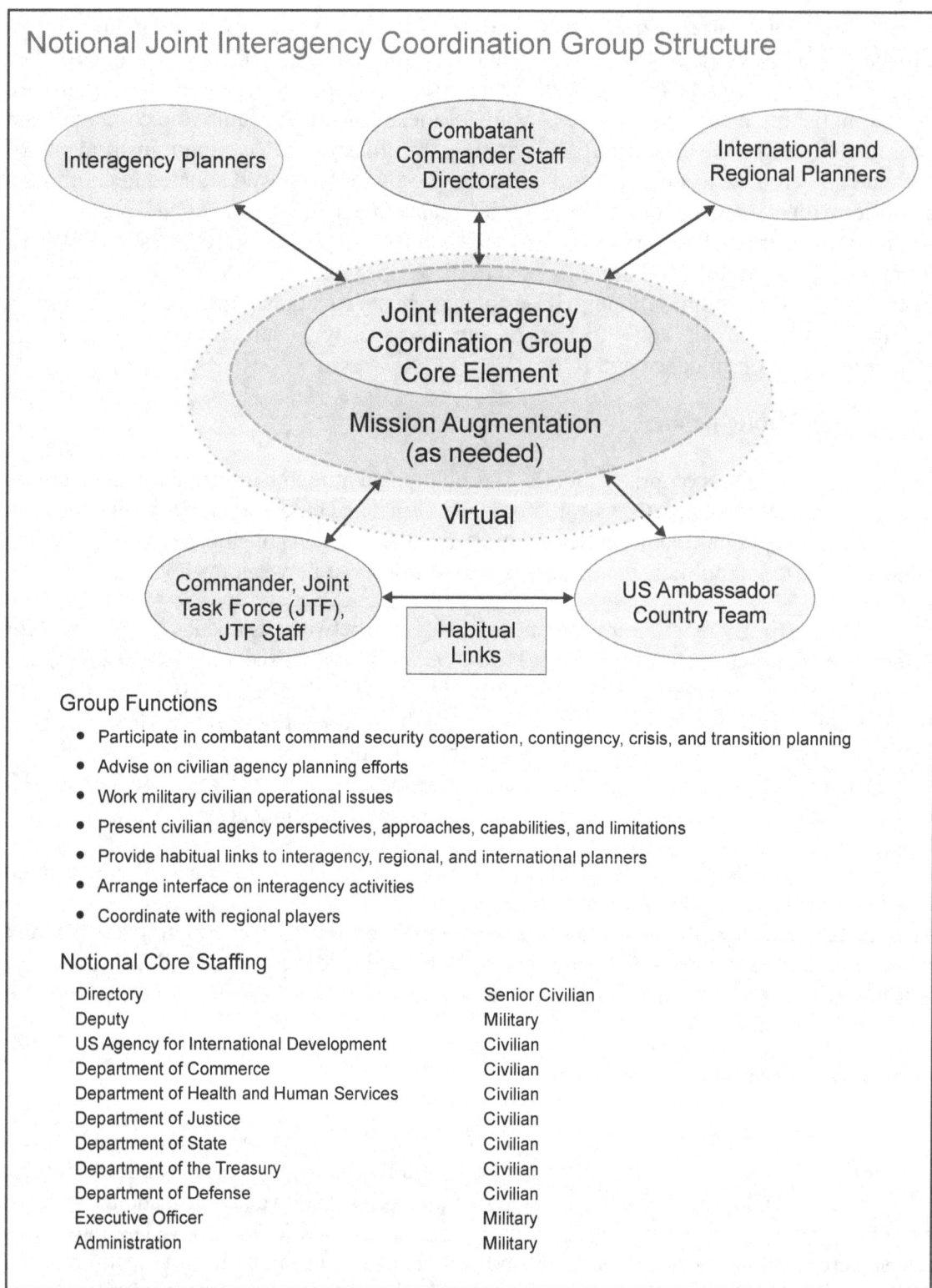

Figure II-4. Notional Joint Interagency Coordination Group Structure

assist in identifying TAs; synchronizing communications media, assets, and messages; and providing news and information to the local population.

(b) Although CMO and IO have much in common, they are distinct disciplines. The TA for much of IO is the adversary; however, the effects of IRCs often reach supporting friendly and neutral populations as well. In a similar vein, CMO seeks to affect friendly and neutral populations, although adversary and potential adversary audiences may also be affected. This being the case, effective integration of CMO with other IRCs is important, and a CMO representative on the IO staff is critical. The regular presence of a CMO representative in the IO cell will greatly promote this level of coordination.

(5) **Cyberspace Operations**

(a) Cyberspace is a global domain within the information environment consisting of the interdependent network of information technology infrastructures and resident data, including the Internet, telecommunications networks, computer systems, and embedded processors and controllers. CO are the employment of cyberspace capabilities where the primary purpose is to achieve objectives in or through cyberspace. Cyberspace capabilities, when in support of IO, deny or manipulate adversary or potential adversary decision making, through targeting an information medium (such as a wireless access point in the physical dimension), the message itself (an encrypted message in the information dimension), or a cyber-persona (an online identity that facilitates communication, decision making, and the influencing of audiences in the cognitive dimension). When employed in support of IO, CO generally focus on the integration of offensive and defensive capabilities exercised in and through cyberspace, in concert with other IRCs, and coordination across multiple lines of operation and lines of effort.

(b) As a process that integrates the employment of IRCs across multiple lines of effort and lines of operation to affect an adversary or potential adversary decision maker, IO can target either the medium (a component within the physical dimension such as a microwave tower) or the message itself (e.g., an encrypted message in the informational dimension). CO is one of several IRCs available to the commander.

For more information, see Joint Publication (JP) 3-12, Cyberspace Operations.

(6) **Information Assurance.** IA is necessary to gain and maintain information superiority. The JFC relies on IA to protect infrastructure to ensure its availability, to position information for influence, and for delivery of information to the adversary. Furthermore, IA and CO are interrelated and rely on each other to support IO.

(7) **Space Operations.** Space capabilities are a significant force multiplier when integrated with joint operations. Space operations support IO through the space force enhancement functions of intelligence, surveillance, and reconnaissance; missile warning; environmental monitoring; satellite communications; and space-based positioning, navigation, and timing. The IO cell is a key place for coordinating and deconflicting the space force enhancement functions with other IRCs.

(8) **Military Information Support Operations.** MISO are planned operations to convey selected information and indicators to foreign audiences to influence their emotions, motives, objective reasoning, and ultimately the behavior of foreign governments,

organizations, groups, and individuals. MISO focuses on the cognitive dimension of the information environment where its TA includes not just potential and actual adversaries, but also friendly and neutral populations. MISO are applicable to a wide range of military operations such as stability operations, security cooperation, maritime interdiction, noncombatant evacuation, foreign humanitarian operations, counterdrug, force protection, and counter-trafficking. Given the wide range of activities in which MISO are employed, the military information support representative within the IO cell should consistently interact with the PA, CMO, JIACG, and IO planners.

(9) Intelligence

(a) Intelligence is a vital military capability that supports IO. The utilization of information operations intelligence integration (IOII) greatly facilitates understanding the interrelationship between the physical, informational, and cognitive dimensions of the information environment.

(b) By providing population-centric socio-cultural intelligence and physical network lay downs, including the information transmitted via those networks, intelligence can greatly assist IRC planners and IO integrators in determining the proper effect to elicit the specific response desired. Intelligence is an integrated process, fusing collection, analysis, and dissemination to provide products that will expose a TA's potential capabilities or vulnerabilities. Intelligence uses a variety of technical and nontechnical tools to assess the information environment, thereby providing insight into a TA.

(c) A joint intelligence support element (JISE) may establish an IO support office (see Figure II-5) to provide IOII. This is due to the long lead time needed to establish information baseline characterizations, provide timely intelligence during IO planning and execution efforts, and to properly assess effects in the information environment. In addition to generating intelligence products to support the IO cell, the JISE IO support office can also work with the JISE collection management office to facilitate development of collection requirements in support of IO assessment efforts.

(10) Military Deception

(a) One of the oldest IRCs used to influence an adversary's perceptions is MILDEC. MILDEC can be characterized as actions executed to deliberately mislead adversary decision makers, creating conditions that will contribute to the accomplishment of the friendly mission. While MILDEC requires a thorough knowledge of an adversary or potential adversary's decision-making processes, it is important to remember that it is focused on desired behavior. It is not enough to simply mislead the adversary or potential adversary; MILDEC is designed to cause them to behave in a manner advantageous to the friendly mission, such as misallocation of resources, attacking at a time and place advantageous to friendly forces, or avoid taking action at all.

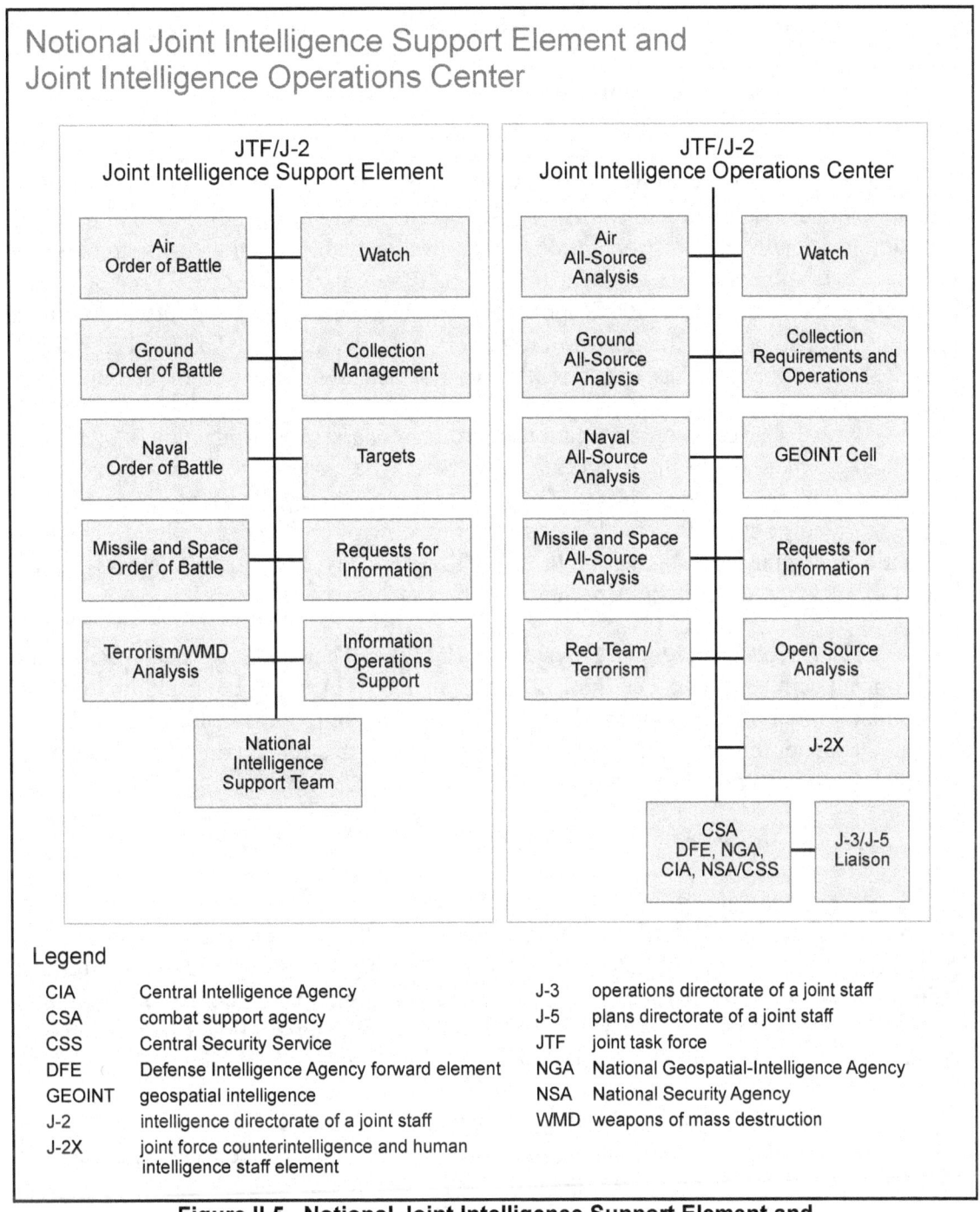

Figure II-5. Notional Joint Intelligence Support Element and Joint Intelligence Operations Center

(b) When integrated with other IRCs, MILDEC can be a particularly powerful way to affect the decision-making processes of an adversary or potential adversary. The IO cell provides a coordinating mechanism for enabling or integrating MILDEC with other IRCs.

(c) MILDEC differs from other IRCs in several ways. Due to the sensitive nature of MILDEC plans, goals, and objectives, a strict need-to-know should be enforced.

(11) **Operations Security**

(a) OPSEC is a standardized process designed to meet operational needs by mitigating risks associated with specific vulnerabilities in order to deny adversaries critical information and observable indicators. OPSEC identifies critical information and actions attendant to friendly military operations to deny observables to adversary intelligence systems. Once vulnerabilities are identified, other IRCs (e.g., MILDEC, CO) can be used to satisfy OPSEC requirements. OPSEC practices must balance the responsibility to account to the American public with the need to protect critical information. The need to practice OPSEC should not be used as an excuse to deny noncritical information to the public.

(b) The effective application, coordination, and synchronization of other IRCs are critical components in the execution of OPSEC. Because a specified IO task is "to protect our own" decision makers, OPSEC planners require complete situational awareness, regarding friendly activities to facilitate the safeguarding of critical information. This kind of situational awareness exists within the IO cell, where a wide range of planners work in concert to integrate and synchronize their actions to achieve a common IO objective.

(12) **Special Technical Operations (STO).** IO need to be deconflicted and synchronized with STO. Detailed information related to STO and its contribution to IO can be obtained from the STO planners at CCMD or Service component headquarters. IO and STO are separate, but have potential crossover, and for this reason an STO planner is a valuable member of the IO cell.

(13) **Joint Electromagnetic Spectrum Operations (JEMSO)**

(a) All information-related mission areas increasingly depend on the electromagnetic spectrum (EMS). JEMSO, consisting of EW and joint EMS management operations, enable EMS-dependent systems to function in their intended operational environment. EW is the mission area ultimately responsible for securing and maintaining freedom of action in the EMS for friendly forces while exploiting or denying it to adversaries. JEMSO therefore supports IO by enabling successful mission area operations.

(b) EW activities are normally planned and managed by personnel dedicated to JEMSO and members of either the joint force commander's electronic warfare staff (JCEWS) or joint electronic warfare cell (EWC). The JCEWS or EWC integrates their efforts into the JFC's targeting cycle and coordinates with, the JFC's IO cell to align objective priorities and help synchronize EW employment with other IRCs.

For more information on EW, see JP 3-13.1, Electronic Warfare. *For more information on JEMSO, see JP 6-01,* Joint Electromagnetic Spectrum Management Operations.

(14) **Key Leader Engagement (KLE)**

(a) KLEs are deliberate, planned engagements between US military leaders and the leaders of foreign audiences that have defined objectives, such as a change in policy or supporting the JFC's objectives. These engagements can be used to shape and influence foreign leaders at the strategic, operational, and tactical levels, and may also be directed toward specific groups such as religious leaders, academic leaders, and tribal leaders; e.g., to solidify trust and confidence in US forces.

(b) KLEs may be applicable to a wide range of operations such as stability operations, counterinsurgency operations, noncombatant evacuation operations, security cooperation activities, and humanitarian operations. When fully integrated with other IRCs into operations, KLEs can effectively shape and influence the leaders of foreign audiences.

b. The capabilities discussed above do not constitute a comprehensive list of all possible capabilities that can contribute to IO. This means that individual capability ownership will be highly diversified. The ability to access these capabilities will be directly related to how well commanders understand and appreciate the importance of IO.

Intentionally Blank

CHAPTER III
AUTHORITIES, RESPONSIBILITIES, AND LEGAL CONSIDERATIONS

> *"Well may the boldest fear and the wisest tremble when incurring responsibilities on which may depend our country's peace and prosperity."*
>
> **President James K. Polk, 1845 Inaugural Address**

1. Introduction

This chapter describes the JFC's authority for the conduct of IO; delineates various roles and responsibilities established in DODD 3600.01, *Information Operations;* and addresses legal considerations in the planning and execution of IO.

2. Authorities

a. The authority to employ IRCs is rooted foremost in Title 10, United States Code (USC). While Title 10, USC, does not specify IO separately, it does provide the legal basis for the roles, missions, and organization of DOD and the Services. Title 10, USC, Section 164, gives command authority over assigned forces to the CCDR, which provides that individual with the authority to organize and employ commands and forces, assign tasks, designate objectives, and provide authoritative direction over all aspects of military operations.

b. DOD and Chairman of the Joint Chiefs of Staff (CJCS) directives delegate authorities to DOD components. Among these directives, DODD 3600.01, *Information Operations*, is the principal IO policy document. Its joint counterpart, Chairman of the Joint Chiefs of Staff Instruction (CJCSI) 3210.01, *Joint Information Operations Policy,* provides joint policy regarding the use of IRCs, professional qualifications for the joint IO force, as well as joint IO education and training requirements. Based upon the contents of these two documents, authority to conduct joint IO is vested in the CCDR, who in turn can delegate operational authority to a subordinate JFC, as appropriate.

c. The nature of IO is such that the exercise of operational authority inherently requires a detailed and rigorous legal interpretation of authority and/or legality of specific actions. Legal considerations are addressed in more detail later in this chapter.

3. Responsibilities

a. **Under Secretary of Defense for Policy (USD[P]).** The USD(P) oversees and manages DOD-level IO programs and activities. In this capacity, USD(P) manages guidance publications (e.g., DODD 3600.01) and all IO policy on behalf of the Secretary of Defense. The office of the USD(P) coordinates IO for all DOD components in the interagency process.

b. **Under Secretary of Defense for Intelligence (USD[I]).** USD(I) develops, coordinates, and oversees the implementation of DOD intelligence policy, programs, and guidance for intelligence activities supporting IO.

c. **Joint Staff.** In accordance with the Secretary of Defense memorandum on *Strategic Communication and Information Operations in the DOD*, dated 25 January 2011, the Joint Staff is assigned the responsibility for joint IO proponency. CJCS responsibilities for IO are both general (such as establishing doctrine, as well as providing advice, and recommendations to the President and Secretary of Defense) and specific (e.g., joint IO policy). As the Joint IO Proponent, the Deputy Director for Global Operations (J-39 DDGO) serves as the CJCS's focal point for IO and coordinates with the Joint Staff, CCMDs, and other organizations that have direct or supporting IO responsibilities. Joint Staff J-39 DDGO also provides IO-related advice and advocacy on behalf of the CCMDs to the CJCS and across DOD. As designated in the Secretary of Defense memorandum on SC and IO, the Joint Staff also serves as the proponent for the IRCs of MILDEC and OPSEC.

d. **Joint Information Operations Warfare Center (JIOWC).** The JIOWC is a CJCS-controlled activity reporting to the operations directorate of a joint staff (J-3) via J-39 DDGO. The JIOWC supports the Joint Staff by ensuring operational integration of IRCs in support of IO, improving DOD's ability to meet CCMD IRC requirements, as well as developing and refining IRCs for use in support of IO across DOD. JIOWC's specific organizational responsibilities include:

(1) Provide IO subject matter experts and advice to the Joint Staff and the CCMDs.

(2) Develop and maintain a joint IO assessment framework.

(3) Assist the Joint IO Proponent in advocating for and integrating CCMD IO requirements.

(4) Upon the direction of the Joint IO Proponent, provide support in coordination and integration of DOD IRCs for JFCs, Service component commanders, and DOD agencies.

e. **Combatant Commands.** The Unified Command Plan provides guidance to CCDRs, assigning them missions and force structure, as well as geographic or functional areas of responsibility. In addition to these responsibilities, the Commander, United States Special Operations Command, is also responsible for integrating and coordinating MISO. This responsibility is focused on enhancing interoperability and providing other CCDRs with MISO planning and execution capabilities. In similar fashion, the Commander, United States Strategic Command (USSTRATCOM) is responsible for advocating on behalf of the IRCs of EW and CO. The Commander, USSTRATCOM, is also focused on enhancing interoperability and providing other CCDRs with contingency EW expertise in support of their missions. For CO, the Commander, USSTRATCOM, synchronizes CO planning. CCDRs integrate, plan, execute, and assess IO when conducting operations or campaigns.

f. **Service Component Commands.** Service component command responsibilities are derived from their parent Service. These responsibilities include recommending to the JFC the proper employment of the Service component IRCs in support of joint IO. The JFC will execute IO using component capabilities.

g. **Functional Component Commands.** Like Service component commands, functional component commands have authority over forces or in the case of IO, IRCs, as delegated by the establishing authority (normally a CCDR or JFC). Functional component commands may be tasked to plan and execute IO as an integrated part of joint operations.

4. Legal Considerations

a. **Introduction.** US military activities in the information environment, as with all military operations, are conducted as a matter of law and policy. Joint IO will always involve legal and policy questions, requiring not just local review, but often national-level coordination and approval. The US Constitution, laws, regulations, and policy, and international law set boundaries for all military activity, to include IO. Whether physically operating from locations outside the US or virtually from any location in the information environment, US forces are required by law and policy to act in accordance with US law and the law of war.

b. **Legal Considerations.** IO planners deal with legal considerations of an extremely diverse and complex nature. Legal interpretations can occasionally differ, given the complexity of technologies involved, the significance of legal interests potentially affected, and the challenges inherent for law and policy to keep pace with the technological changes and implementation of IRCs. Additionally, policies are regularly added, amended, and rescinded in an effort to provide clarity. As a result, IO remains a dynamic arena, which can be further complicated by multinational operations, as each nation has its own laws, policies, and processes for approving plans. The brief discussion in this publication is not a substitute for sound legal advice regarding specific IRC- and IO-related activities. For this reason, joint IO planners should consult their staff judge advocate or legal advisor for expert advice.

c. **Implications Beyond the JFC.** Bilateral agreements to which the US is a signatory may have provisions concerning the conduct of IO as well as IRCs when they are used in support of IO. IO planners at all levels should consider the following broad areas within each planning iteration in consultation with the appropriate legal advisor:

(1) Could the execution of a particular IRC be considered a hostile act by an adversary or potential adversary?

(2) Do any non-US laws concerning national security, privacy, or information exchange, criminal and/or civil issues apply?

(3) What are the international treaties, agreements, or customary laws recognized by an adversary or potential adversary that apply to IRCs?

(4) How is the joint force interacting with or being supported by US intelligence organizations and other interagency entities?

Intentionally Blank

CHAPTER IV
INTEGRATING INFORMATION-RELATED CAPABILITIES INTO THE JOINT OPERATION PLANNING PROCESS

> *"Support planning is conducted in parallel with other planning and encompasses such essential factors as IO [information operations], SC [strategic communication]..."*
>
> **Joint Publication 5-0, *Joint Operation Planning*, 11 August 2011**

1. Introduction

The IO cell chief is responsible to the JFC for integrating IRCs into the joint operation planning process (JOPP). Thus, the IO staff is responsible for coordinating and synchronizing IRCs to accomplish the JFC's objectives. Coordinated IO are essential in employing the elements of operational design. Conversely, uncoordinated IO efforts can compromise, complicate, negate, and pose risks to the successful accomplishment of the JFC and USG objectives. Additionally, when uncoordinated, other USG and/or multinational information activities, may complicate, defeat, or render DOD IO ineffective. For this reason, the JFC's objectives require early detailed IO staff planning, coordination, and deconfliction between the USG and partner nations' efforts within the AOR, in order to effectively synchronize and integrate IRCs.

2. Information Operations Planning

a. **The IO cell and the JPG.** The IO cell chief ensures joint IO planners adequately represent the IO cell within the JPG and other JFC planning processes. Doing so will help ensure that IRCs are integrated with all planning efforts. Joint IO planners should be integrated with the joint force planning, directing, monitoring, and assessing process.

b. **IO Planning Considerations**

(1) IO planners seek to create an operational advantage that results in coordinated effects that directly support the JFC's objectives. IRCs can be executed throughout the operational environment, but often directly impact the content and flow of information.

(2) IO planning begins at the **earliest stage** of JOPP and must be an integral part of, not an addition to, the overall planning effort. IRCs can be used in all phases of a campaign or operation, but their effective employment during the shape and deter phases can have a significant impact on remaining phases.

(3) The use of IO to achieve the JFC's objectives requires the ability to integrate IRCs and interagency support into a comprehensive and coherent strategy that supports the JFC's overall mission objectives. The GCC's theater security cooperation guidance contained in the theater campaign plan (TCP) serves as an excellent platform to embed specific long-term information objectives during phase 0 operations. For this reason, the IO

staff and IO cell should work closely with their plans directorate staff as well as the JIACG in the development of the security cooperation portion of the TCP.

(4) Many IRCs require long lead time for development of the joint intelligence preparation of the operational environment (JIPOE) and release authority. The intelligence directorate of a joint staff (J-2) identifies intelligence and information gaps, shortfalls, and priorities as part of the JIPOE process in the early stages of the JOPP. Concurrently, the IO cell must identify similar intelligence gaps in its understanding of the information environment to determine if it has sufficient information to successfully plan IO. Where identified shortfalls exist, the IO cell may need to work with J-2 to submit requests for information (RFIs) to the J-2 to fill gaps that cannot be filled internally.

(5) There may be times where the JFC may lack sufficient detailed intelligence data and intelligence staff personnel to provide IOII. Similarly, a JFC's staff may lack dedicated resources to provide support. For this reason, it is imperative the IO cell take a proactive approach to intelligence support. The IO cell must also review and provide input to the commander's critical information requirements (CCIRs), especially priority intelligence requirements (PIRs) and information requirements. The joint intelligence staff, using PIRs as a basis, develops information requirements that are most critical. These are also known as essential elements of information (EEIs). In the course of mission analysis, the intelligence analyst identifies the intelligence required to CCIRs. Intelligence staffs develop more specific questions known as information requirements. EEIs pertinent to the IO staff may include target information specifics, such as messages and counter-messages, adversary propaganda, and responses of individuals, groups, and organizations to adversary propaganda.

(6) As part of JOPP, designation of release and execution authorities for IRCs is required. For example, release authority provides approval for the employment of specific IRCs in support of a commander's objectives and normally specifies the allocation of specific offensive means and IRCs. For its part, the execution authority constitutes the authority to employ IRCs. Normally, the JFC is designated in the execution order as the execution authority. Given the fact that IRC effects are often required across multiple operational phases, each capability requires separate and distinct authorities.

c. **IO and the Joint Operation Planning Process**

Throughout JOPP, IRCs are integrated with the JFC's overall CONOPS (see Figure IV-1). An overview of the seven steps of JOPP follow; however, a more detailed discussion of the planning process can be found in JP 5-0, *Joint Operation Planning*.

(1) **Planning Initiation.** Integration of IRCs into joint operations should begin at step 1, planning initiation. Key IO staff actions during this step include the following:

(a) Review key strategic documents.

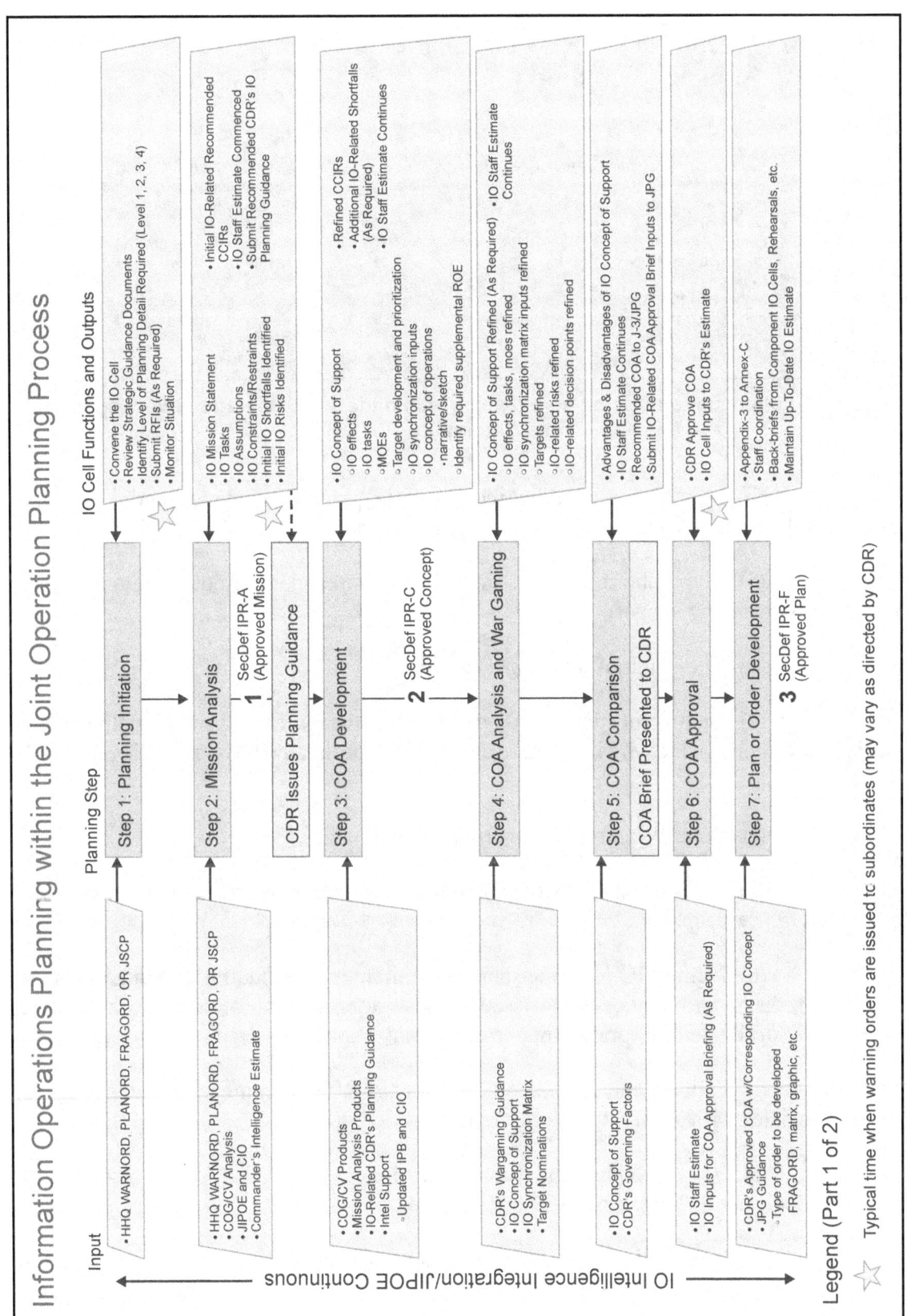

Figure IV-1. Information Operations Planning within the Joint Operation Planning Process

```
Information Operations Planning within the Joint Operation
Planning Process (continued)

Legend (Part 2 of 2)

CCIR       commander's critical information requirement    J-3        operations directorate of a joint staff
CDR        commander                                        JIPOE      joint intelligence preparation of the
CIO        combined information overlay                                operational environment
COA        course of action                                 JPG        joint planning group
COG        center of gravity                                JSCP       Joint Strategic Capabilities Plan
CV         critical vulnerability                           MOE        measure of effectiveness
FRAGORD    fragmentary order                                PLANORD    planning order
HHQ        higher headquarters                              RFI        request for information
IPB        intelligence preparation of the battlespace      ROE        rules of engagement
IPR        in-progress review                               SecDef     Secretary of Defense
IO         information operations                           WARNORD    warning order
```

Figure IV-1. Information Operations Planning within the Joint Operation Planning Process (cont'd)

(b) Monitor the situation, receive initial planning guidance, and review staff estimates from applicable operation plans (OPLANs) and concept plans (CONPLANs).

(c) Alert subordinate and supporting commanders of potential tasking with regard to IO planning support.

(d) Gauge initial scope of IO required for the operation.

(e) Identify location, standard operating procedures, and battle rhythm of other staff organizations that require integration and divide coordination responsibilities among the IO staff.

(f) Identify and request appropriate authorities.

(g) Begin identifying information required for mission analysis and course of action (COA) development.

(h) Identify IO planning support requirements (including staff augmentation, support products, and services) and issue requests for support according to procedures established locally and by various supporting organizations.

(i) Validate, initiate, and revise PIRs and RFIs, keeping in mind the long lead times associated with satisfying IO requirements.

(j) Provide IO input and recommendations to COAs, and provide resolutions to conflicts that exist with other plans or lines of operation.

(k) In coordination with the targeting cell, submit potential candidate targets to JFC or component joint targeting coordination board (JTCB). For vetting, validation, and deconfliction follow local targeting cell procedures because these three separate processes do not always occur at the JTCB.

(l) Ensure IO staff and IO cell members participate in all JFC or component planning and targeting sessions and JTCBs.

(2) **Mission Analysis.** The purpose of step 2, mission analysis, is to understand the problem and purpose of an operation and issue the appropriate guidance to drive the remaining steps of the planning process. The end state of mission analysis is a clearly defined mission and thorough staff assessment of the joint operation. Mission analysis orients the JFC and staff on the problem and develops a common understanding, before moving forward in the planning process. During mission analysis, all staff sections, including the IO cell, will examine the mission from their own functional perspective and contribute the results of that analysis to the JPG. As IO impacts each element of the operational environment, it is important for the IO staff and IO cell during mission analysis to remain focused on the information environment. Key IO staff actions during mission analysis are:

(a) Assist the J-3 and J-2 in the identification of friendly and adversary center(s) of gravity and critical factors (e.g., critical capabilities, critical requirements, and critical vulnerabilities).

(b) Identify relevant aspects of the physical, informational, and cognitive dimensions (whether friendly, neutral, adversary, or potential adversary) of the information environment.

(c) Identify specified, implied, and essential tasks.

(d) Identify facts, assumptions, constraints, and restraints affecting IO planning.

(e) Analyze IRCs available to support IO and authorities required for their employment.

(f) Develop and refine proposed PIRs, RFIs, and CCIRs.

(g) Conduct initial IO-related risk assessment.

(h) Develop IO mission statement.

(i) Begin developing the initial IO staff estimate. This estimate forms the basis for the IO cell chief's recommendation to the JFC, regarding which COA it can best support.

(j) Conduct initial force allocation review.

(k) Identify and develop potential targets and coordinate with the targeting cell no later than the end of target development. Compile and maintain target folders in the Modernized Integrated Database. Coordinate with the J-2 and targeting cell for participation and representation in vetting, validation, and targeting boards (e.g., JTCB, joint targeting working group).

(l) Develop mission success criteria.

(3) **COA Development.** Output from mission analysis, such as initial staff estimates, mission and tasks, and JFC planning guidance are used in step 3, COA development. Key IO staff actions during this step include the following:

(a) Identify desired and undesired effects that support or degrade JFC's information objectives.

(b) Develop measures of effectiveness (MOEs) and measures of effectiveness indicators (MOEIs).

(c) Develop tasks for recommendation to the J-3.

(d) Recommend IRCs that may be used to accomplish supporting information tasks for each COA.

(e) Analyze required supplemental rules of engagement (ROE).

(f) Identify additional operational risks and controls/mitigation.

(g) Develop the IO CONOPS narrative/sketch.

(h) Synchronize IRCs in time, space, and purpose.

(i) Continue update/development of the IO staff estimate.

(j) Prepare inputs to the COA brief.

(k) Provide inputs to the target folder.

(4) **COA Analysis and War Gaming.** Based upon time available, the JFC staff should war game each tentative COA against adversary COAs identified through the JIPOE process. Key IO staff and IO cell actions during this step include the following:

(a) Analyze each COA from an IO functional perspective.

(b) Reveal key decision points.

(c) Recommend task adjustments to IRCs as appropriate.

(d) Provide IO-focused data for use in a synchronization matrix or other decision-making tool.

(e) Identify IO portions of branches and sequels.

(f) Identify possible high-value targets related to IO.

(g) Submit PIRs and recommend CCIRs for IO.

(h) Revise staff estimate.

(i) Assess risk.

(5) **COA Comparison.** Step 5, COA comparison, starts with all staff elements analyzing and evaluating the advantages and disadvantages of each COA from their respective viewpoints. Key IO staff and IO cell actions during this step include the following:

(a) Compare each COA based on mission and tasks.

(b) Compare each COA in relation to IO requirements versus available IRCs.

(c) Prioritize COAs from an IO perspective.

(d) Revise the IO staff estimate. During execution, the IO cell should maintain an estimate and update as required.

(6) **COA Approval.** Just like other elements of the JFC's staff, during step 6, COA approval, the IO staff provides the JFC with a clear recommendation of how IO can best contribute to mission accomplishment in the COA(s) being briefed. It is vital this recommendation is presented in a clear, concise manner that is not only able to be quickly grasped by the JFC, but can also be easily understood by peer, subordinate, and higher-headquarters command and staff elements. Failure to foster such an understanding of IO contribution to the approved COA can lead to poor execution and/or coordination of IRCs in subsequent operations.

(7) **Plan or Order Development.** Once a COA is selected and approved, the IO staff develops appendix 3 (Information Operations) to annex C (Operations) of the operation order (OPORD) or OPLAN. Because IRC integration is documented elsewhere in the OPORD or OPLAN, it is imperative that the IO staff conduct effective staff coordination within the JPG during step 7, plan or order development. Key staff actions during this step include the following:

(a) Refine tasks from the approved COA.

(b) Identify shortfalls of IRCs and recommend solutions.

(c) Facilitate development of supporting plans by keeping the responsible organizations informed of relevant details (as access restrictions allow) throughout the planning process.

(d) Advise the supported commander on IO issues and concerns during the supporting plan review and approval process.

(e) Participate in time-phased force and deployment data refinement to ensure IO supports the OPLAN or CONPLAN.

(f) Assist in the development of OPLAN or CONPLAN appendix 6 (IO Intelligence Integration) to annex B (Intelligence).

d. **Plan Refinement.** The information environment is continuously changing and it is critical for IO planners to remain in constant interaction with the JPG to provide updates to OPLANs or CONPLANs.

e. **Assessment of IO.** Assessment is integrated into all phases of the planning and execution cycle, and consists of assessment activities associated with tasks, events, or programs in support of joint military operations. Assessment seeks to analyze and inform on the performance and effectiveness of activities. The intent is to provide relevant feedback to decision makers in order to modify activities that achieve desired results. Assessment can also provide the programmatic community with relevant information that informs on return on investment and operational effectiveness of DOD IRCs. It is important to note that integration of assessment into planning is the first step of the assessment process. Planning for assessment is part of broader operational planning, rather than an afterthought. Iterative in nature, assessment supports the Adaptive Planning and Execution process, and provides feedback to operations and ultimately, IO enterprise programmatics.

For more on assessments, see JP 5-0, Joint Operation Planning.

f. **Relationship Between Measures of Performance (MOPs) and MOEs.** Effectiveness assessment is one of the greatest challenges facing a staff. Despite the continuing evolution of joint and Service doctrine and the refinement of supporting tactics, techniques, and procedures, assessing the effectiveness of IRCs continues to be challenging. MOEs attempt to accomplish this assessment by quantifying the intangible attributes within the information environment, in order to assess the effectiveness of IRCs against an adversary or potential adversary. Figures IV-2 and IV-3 are tangible examples of MOP and MOE sources that an IO planner would have to rely on for feedback.

(1) MOPs are criteria used to assess friendly accomplishment of tasks and mission execution.

Examples of Measures of Performance Feedback

- Numbers of populace listening to military information support operations (MISO) broadcasts

- Percentage of adversary command and control facilities attacked

- Number of civil-military operations projects initiated/number of projects completed

- Human intelligence reports number of MISO broadcasts during Commando Solo missions

---

Figure IV-2. Examples of Measures of Performance Feedback

Possible Sources of Measures of Effectiveness Feedback

- Intelligence assessments (human intelligence, etc.)
- Open source intelligence
- Internet (newsgroups, etc.)
- Military information support operations, and civil-military operations teams (face to face activities)
- Contact with the public
- Press inquiries and comments
- Department of State polls, reports and surveys (reports)
- Open Source Center
- Nongovernmental organizations, intergovernmental organizations, international organizations, and host nation organizations
- Foreign policy advisor meetings
- Commercial polls
- Operational analysis cells

Figure IV-3. Possible Sources of Measures of Effectiveness Feedback

(2) In contrast to MOPs, MOEs are criteria used to assess changes in system behavior, capability, or operational environment that are tied to measuring the attainment of an end state, achievement of an objective, or creation of an effect. Ultimately, MOEs determine whether actions being executed are creating desired effects, thereby accomplishing the JFC's information objectives and end state.

(3) MOEs and MOPs are both crafted and refined throughout JOPP. In developing MOEs and/or MOPs, the following general criteria should be considered:

(a) **Ends Related.** MOEs and/or MOPs should directly relate to the objectives and desired tasks required to accomplish effects and/or performance.

(b) **Measurable.** MOEs should be *specific, measurable,* and *observable.* Effectiveness or performance is measured either quantitatively (e.g., counting the number of attacks) or qualitatively (e.g., subjectively evaluating the level of confidence in the security forces). In the case of MOEs, **a baseline measurement must be established prior to the execution, against which to measure system changes.**

(c) **Timely.** A time for required feedback should be clearly stated for each MOE and/or MOP and a plan made to report within that specified time period.

(d) **Properly Resourced.** The collection, analysis, and reporting of MOE or MOP data requires personnel, financial, and materiel resources. The IO staff or IO cell should ensure that these resource requirements are built into IO planning during COA development and closely coordinated with the J-2 collection manager to ensure the means to assess these measures are in place.

(4) **Measure of Effectiveness Indicators.** An MOEI is a unit, location, or event observed or measured, that can be used to assess an MOE. These are often used to add quantitative data points to qualitative MOEs and can assist an IO staff or IO cell in answering a question related to a qualitative MOE. The identification of MOEIs aids the IO staff or IO cell in determining an MOE and can be identified from across the information environment. MOEIs can be independently weighted for their contribution to an MOE and should be based on separate criteria. Hundreds of MOEIs may be needed for a large scale contingency. Examples of how effects can be translated into MOEIs include the following:

(a) **Effect:** Increase in the city populace's participation in civil governance.

1. **MOE:** (Qualitative) Metropolitan citizens display increased support for the democratic leadership elected on 1 July. (What activity trends show progress toward or away from the desired behavior?)

2. **MOEI:**

a. A decrease in the number of anti-government rallies/demonstrations in a city since 1 July (this indicator might be weighted heavily at 60 percent of this MOE's total assessment based on rallies/demonstrations observed.)

b. An increase in the percentage of positive new government media stories since 1 July (this indicator might be weighted less heavily at 20 percent of this MOE's total assessment based on media monitoring.)

c. An increase in the number of citizens participating in democratic functions since 1 July (this indicator might be weighted at 20 percent of this MOE's total assessment based on government data/criteria like voter registration, city council meeting attendance, and business license registration.)

(b) **Effect:** Insurgent leadership does not orchestrate terrorist acts in the western region.

1. **MOE:** (Qualitative) Decrease in popular support toward extremists and insurgents.

2. **MOEI:**

a. An increase in the number of insurgents turned in/identified since 1 October.

b. An increase in the amount of money disbursed to citizens from the "rewards program" since 1 October.

<u>c.</u> The percentage of blogs supportive of the local officials.

3. Information Operations Phasing and Synchronization

Through its contributions to the GCC's TCP, it is clear that joint IO is expected to play a major role in all phases of joint operations. This means that the GCC's IO staff and IO cell must account for logical transitions from phase to phase, as joint IO moves from the main effort to a supporting effort. Regardless of what operational phase may be underway, it is always important for the IO staff and IO cell to determine what legal authorities the JFC requires to execute IRCs during the subsequent operations phase.

a. **Phase 0–Shape.** Joint IO planning should focus on supporting the TCP to deter adversaries and potential adversaries from posing significant threats to US objectives. Joint IO planners should access the JIACG through the IO cell or staff. Joint IO planning during this phase will need to prioritize and integrate efforts and resources to support activities throughout the interagency. Due to competing resources and the potential lack of available IRCs, executing joint IO during phase 0 can be challenging. For this reason, the IO staff and IO cell will need to consider how their IO activities fit in as part of a whole-of-government approach to effectively shape the information environment to achieve the CCDR's information objectives.

b. **Phase I–Deter.** During this phase, joint IO is often the main effort for the CCMD. Planning will likely emphasize the JFC's flexible deterrent options (FDOs), complementing US public diplomacy efforts, in order to influence a potential foreign adversary decision maker to make decisions favorable to US goals and objectives. Joint IO planning for this phase is especially complicated because the FDO typically must have a chance to work, while still allowing for a smooth transition to phase II and more intense levels of conflict, if it does not. Because the transition from phase I to phase II may not allow enough time for application of IRCs to create the desired effects on an adversary or potential adversary, the phase change may be abrupt.

c. **Phase II-Seize Initiative.** In phase II, joint IO is supporting multiple lines of operation. Joint IO planning during phase II should focus on maximizing synchronized IRC effects to support the JFC's objectives and the component missions while preparing the transition to the next phase.

d. **Phase III–Dominate.** Joint IO can be a supporting and/or a supported line of operation during phase III. Joint IO planning during phase III will involve developing an information advantage across multiple lines of operation to execute the mission.

e. **Phase IV–Stabilize.** CMO, or even IO, is likely the supported line of operation during phase IV. Joint IO planning during this phase will need to be flexible enough to simultaneously support CMO and combat operations. As the US military and interagency information activity capacity matures and eventually slows, the JFC should assist the host-nation security forces and government information capacity to resume and expand, as necessary. As host nation information capacity improves, the JFC should be able to refocus joint IO efforts to other mission areas. Expanding host-nation capacity through military and interagency efforts will help foster success in the next phase.

    f. **Phase V-Enable Civil Authority.** During phase V, joint IO planning focuses on supporting the redeployment of US forces, as well as providing continued support to stability operations. IO planning during phase V should account for interagency and country team efforts to resume the lead mission for information within the host nation territory. The IO staff and cell can anticipate the possibility of long term US commercial and government support to the former adversary's economic and political interests to continue through the completion of this phase.

CHAPTER V
MULTINATIONAL INFORMATION OPERATIONS

"In order more effectively to achieve the objectives of this Treaty, the Parties, separately and jointly, by means of continuous and effective self-help and mutual aid, will maintain and develop their individual and collective capacity to resist armed attack."

Article 3, The North Atlantic Treaty, April 4, 1949

1. Introduction

Joint doctrine for multinational operations, including command and operations in a multinational environment, is described in JP 3-16, *Multinational Operations*. The purpose of this chapter is to highlight specific doctrinal components of IO in a multinational environment (see Figure V-1). In doing so, this chapter will build upon those aspects of IO addressed in JP 3-16. Additional data regarding IO in a multinational environment can be found in Allied Joint Publication (AJP)-3.10, *Allied Joint Doctrine for Information Operations*. This chapter includes IO coordination processes, staff requirements, planning formats, and matrices for staff and commanders involved in a multinational operation.

Information Operations in the Multinational Environment

Figure V-1. Information Operations in the Multinational Environment

2. Other Nations and Information Operations

a. Multinational partners recognize a variety of information concepts and possess sophisticated doctrine, procedures, and capabilities. Given these potentially diverse perspectives regarding IO, it is essential for the multinational force commander (MNFC) to resolve potential conflicts as soon as possible. It is vital to integrate multinational partners into IO planning as early as possible to gain agreement on an integrated and achievable IO strategy. Initial requirements for coordinating, synchronizing, and when required integrating other nations into the US IO plan include:

(1) Clarifying all multinational partner information objectives.

(2) Understanding all multinational partner employment of IRCs.

(3) Establishing IO deconfliction procedures to avoid conflicting messages.

(4) Identifying multinational force (MNF) vulnerabilities as soon as possible.

(5) Developing a strategy to mitigate MNF IO vulnerabilities.

(6) Identifying MNF IRCs.

b. Regardless of the maturity of each partner's IO strategy, doctrine, capabilities, tactics, techniques, or procedures, every multinational partner can contribute to MNF IO by providing regional expertise to assist in planning and conducting IO. Multinational partners have developed unique approaches to IO that are tailored for specific targets in ways that may not be employed by the US. Such contributions complement US IO expertise and IRCs, potentially enhancing the quality of both the planning and execution of multinational IO.

3. Multinational Information Operations Considerations

a. Military operation planning processes, particularly for IO, whether JOPP based or based on established or agreed to multinational planning processes, include an understanding of multinational partner(s):

(1) Cultural values and institutions.

(2) Interests and concerns.

(3) Moral and ethical values.

(4) ROE and legal constraints.

(5) Challenges in multilingual planning for the employment of IRCs.

(6) IO doctrine, techniques, and procedures.

b. Sharing of information with multinational partners.

(1) Each nation has various IRCs to provide, in support of multinational objectives. These nations are obliged to protect information that they cannot share across the MNF. However, to plan thoroughly, all nations must be willing to share appropriate information to accomplish the assigned mission.

(2) Information sharing arrangements in formal alliances, to include US participation in United Nations missions, are worked out as part of alliance protocols. Information sharing arrangements in ad hoc multinational operations where coalitions are working together on a short-notice mission must be created during the establishment of the coalition.

(3) Using National Disclosure Policy (NDP) 1, *National Policy and Procedures for the Disclosure of Classified Military Information to Foreign Governments and International Organizations*, and Department of Defense Instruction (DODI) O-3600.02, *Information Operations (IO) Security Classification Guidance (U)*, as guidance, the senior US commander in a multinational operation must provide guidelines to the US-designated disclosure representative on information sharing and the release of classified information or capabilities to the MNF. NDP 1 provides policy and procedures in the form of specific disclosure criteria and limitations, definition of terms, release arrangements, and other guidance. The disclosure of classified information is never automatic. It is not necessary for MNFs to be made aware of all US intelligence, capabilities, or procedures that are required for planning and execution of IO. The JFC should request approval from higher command authorities to release information that has not been previously cleared for multinational partners.

(4) Information concerning US persons may only be collected, retained, or disseminated in accordance with law and regulation. Applicable provisions include: the Privacy Act, Title 5, USC, Section 552a; DODD 5200.27, *Acquisition of Information Concerning Persons and Organizations not Affiliated with the Department of Defense*; Executive Order 12333, *United States Intelligence Activities*; and DOD 5240.1-R, *Procedures Governing the Activities of DOD Intelligence Components that Affect United States Persons*.

4. Planning, Integration, and Command and Control of Information Operations in Multinational Operations

a. The role of IO in multinational operations is the prerogative of the MNFC. The mission of the MNF determines the role of IO in each specific operation.

b. Representation of key multinational partners in the MNF IO cell allows their expertise and capabilities to be utilized, and the IO portion of the plan to be better coordinated and more timely.

c. While some multinational partners may not have developed an IO concept or fielded IRCs, it is important that they fully appreciate the importance of the information in achieving the MNFC's objectives. For this reason, every effort should be made to provide basic-level IO training to multinational partners serving on the MNF IO staff. In cases where this is not possible, it may be necessary for the MNF headquarters staff to assist the subordinate MNFCs in planning and conducting IO.

d. MNF headquarters staff could be organized differently; however, as a general rule, an information operations coordination board (IOCB) or similar organization may exist (see Figure V-2). The IOCB is normally responsible for preparing inputs to relevant MNF headquarters internal and external processes such as joint targeting and provides a forum to outline current and future application of IRCs designed to achieve MNFC's objectives. A wide range of MNF headquarters staff organizations should participate in IOCB deliberations to ensure their input and subject matter expertise can be applied to satisfy a requirement in order to achieve MNFC's objectives.

e. Besides the coordination activities highlighted above, the IOCB should also participate in appropriate joint operations planning groups (JOPGs) and should take part in early discussions, including mission analysis. An IO presence on the JOPG is essential, as it is the IOCB which provides input to the overall estimate process in close coordination with other members of the MNF headquarters staff.

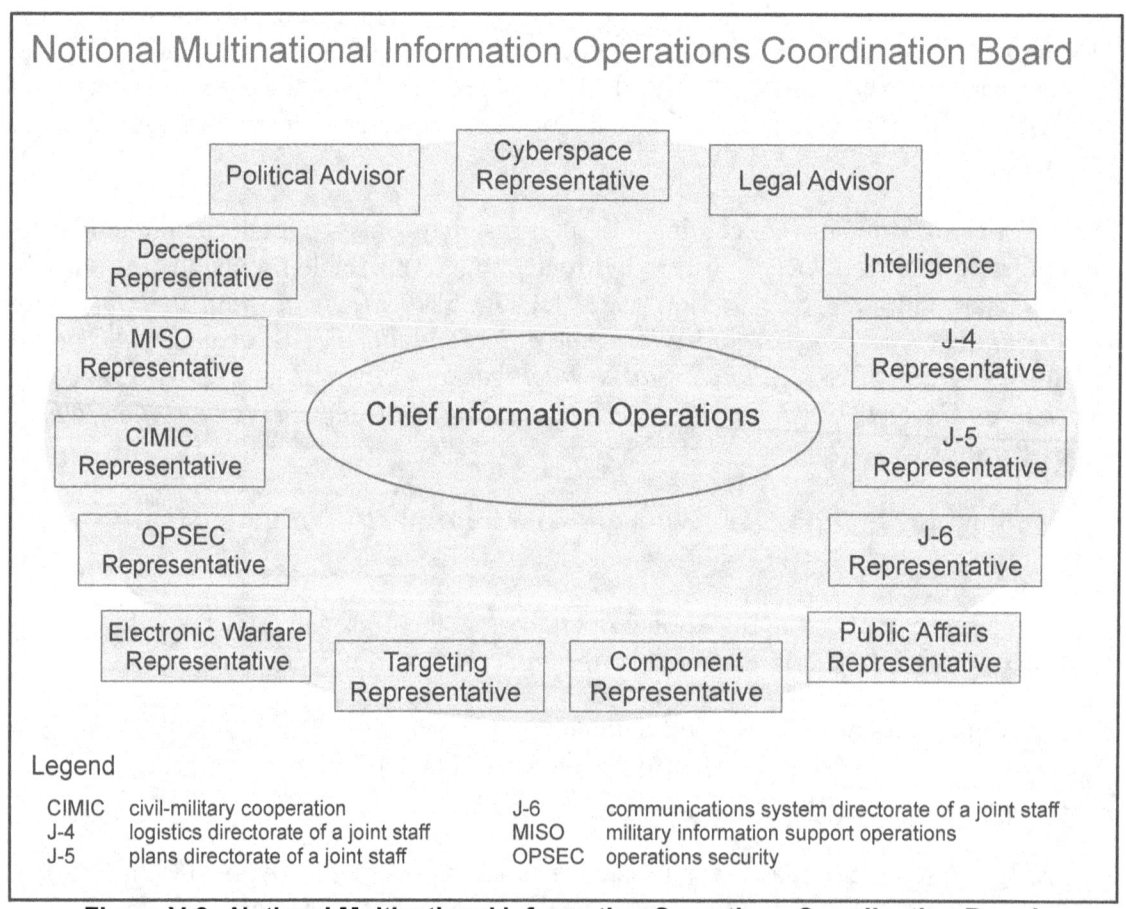

Figure V-2. Notional Multinational Information Operations Coordination Board

5. Multinational Organization for Information Operations Planning

a. When the JFC is also the MNFC, the joint force staff should be augmented by planners and subject matter experts from the MNF. MNF IO planners and IRC specialists should be trained on US and MNF doctrine, requirements, resources, and how the MNF is structured to integrate IRCs. IO planners should seek to accommodate the requirements of each multinational partner, within given constraints, with the goal of using all the available expertise and capabilities of the MNF.

b. In the case where the JFC is not the MNFC, it may be necessary for **the J-3 to brief the MNFC and staff on the advantages of integrating US IO processes and procedures to achieve MNF objectives.** The JFC should propose organizing a multinational IO staff using organizational criteria discussed earlier. If this is not acceptable to the MNFC, the JFC should assume responsibility for implementing IO within the joint force as a part of multinational operations to support multinational mission objectives.

6. Multinational Policy Coordination

The development of capabilities, tactics, techniques, procedures, plans, intelligence, and communications support applicable to IO requires coordination with the responsible DOD components and multinational partners. Coordination with partner nations above the JFC/MNFC level is normally effected within existing defense arrangements, including bilateral arrangements. **The Joint Staff coordinates US positions on IO matters** delegated to them as a matter of law or policy, and discusses them bilaterally, or in multinational organizations, to achieve interoperability and compatibility in fulfilling common requirements. Direct discussions regarding multinational IO planning in specific theaters are the responsibility of the GCC.

Intentionally Blank

APPENDIX A
REFERENCES

The development of JP 3-13 is based on the following primary references.

1. General

   a. *National Security Strategy.*

   b. *Unified Command Plan.*

   c. Executive Order 12333, *United States Intelligence Activities.*

   d. The Fourth Amendment to the US Constitution.

   e. *The Privacy Act,* Title 5, USC, Section 552a.

   f. *The Wiretap Act and the Pen/Trap Statute,* Title 18, USC, Sections 2510-2522 and 3121-3127.

   g. *The Stored Communications Act,* Title 18, USC, Sections 2701-2712.

   h. *The Foreign Intelligence Surveillance Act,* Title 50, USC.

2. Department of State Publications

Department of State Publication 9434, *Treaties In Force.*

3. Department of Defense Publications

   a. Secretary of Defense Memorandum dated 25 January 2011, *Strategic Communication and Information Operations in the DOD.*

   b. *National Military Strategy.*

   c. DODD S-3321.1, *Overt Psychological Operations Conducted by the Military Services in Peacetime and in Contingencies Short of Declared War.*

   d. DODD 3600.01, *Information Operations (IO).*

   e. DODD 5200.27, *Acquisition of Information Concerning Persons and Organizations not Affiliated with the Department of Defense.*

   f. DOD 5240.1-R, *Procedures Governing the Activities of DOD Intelligence Components that Affect United States Persons.*

   g. DODI O-3600.02, *Information Operation (IO) Security Classification Guidance.*

4. Chairman of the Joint Chiefs of Staff Publications

a. CJCSI 1800.01D, *Officer Professional Military Education Policy (OPMEP)*.

b. CJCSI 3141.01E, *Management and Review of Joint Strategic Capabilities Plan (JSCP)-Tasked Plans*.

c. CJCSI 3150.25E, *Joint Lessons Learned Program*.

d. CJCSI 3210.01B, *Joint Information Operations Policy*.

e. Chairman of the Joint Chiefs of Staff Manual (CJCSM) 3122.01A, *Joint Operation Planning and Execution System (JOPES) Volume I, Planning Policies and Procedures*.

f. CJCSM 3122.02D, *Joint Operation Planning and Execution System (JOPES) Volume III, Time-Phased Force and Deployment Data Development and Deployment Execution*.

g. CJCSM 3122.03C, *Joint Operation Planning and Execution System (JOPES) Volume II, Planning Formats*.

h. CJCSM 3500.03C, *Joint Training Manual for the Armed Forces of the United States*.

i. CJCSM 3500.04F, *Universal Joint Task Manual*.

j. JP 1, *Doctrine for the Armed Forces of the United States*.

k. JP 1-02, *Department of Defense Dictionary of Military and Associated Terms*.

l. JP 1-04, *Legal Support to Military Operations*.

m. JP 2-0, *Joint Intelligence*.

n. JP 2-01, *Joint and National Intelligence Support to Military Operations*.

o. JP 2-01.3, *Joint Intelligence Preparation of the Operational Environment*.

p. JP 2-03, *Geospatial Intelligence Support to Joint Operations*.

q. JP 3-0, *Joint Operations*.

r. JP 3-08, *Interorganizational Coordination During Joint Operations*.

s. JP 3-10, *Joint Security Operations in Theater*.

t. JP 3-12, *Cyberspace Operations*.

u. JP 3-13.1, *Electronic Warfare*.

v. JP 3-13.2, *Military Information Support Operations*.

w. JP 3-13.3, *Operations Security*.

x. JP 3-13.4, *Military Deception*.

y. JP 3-14, *Space Operations*.

z. JP 3-16, *Multinational Operations*.

aa. JP 3-57, *Civil-Military Operations*.

bb. JP 3-60, *Joint Targeting*.

cc. JP 3-61, *Public Affairs*.

dd. JP 5-0, *Joint Operation Planning*.

ee. JP 6-01, *Joint Electromagnetic Spectrum Management Operations*.

5. Multinational Publication

AJP 3-10, *Allied Joint Doctrine for Information Operations*.

Intentionally Blank

APPENDIX B
ADMINISTRATIVE INSTRUCTIONS

1. User Comments

Users in the field are highly encouraged to submit comments on this publication to: Joint Staff J-7, Deputy Director, Joint and Coalition Warfighting, Joint and Coalition Warfighting Center, ATTN: Joint Doctrine Support Division, 116 Lake View Parkway, Suffolk, VA 23435-2697. These comments should address content (accuracy, usefulness, consistency, and organization), writing, and appearance.

2. Authorship

The lead agent and the Joint Staff doctrine sponsor for this publication is the Director for Operations (J-3).

3. Supersession

This publication supersedes JP 3-13, 13 February 2006, *Information Operations*.

4. Change Recommendations

a. Recommendations for urgent changes to this publication should be submitted:

TO: JOINT STAFF WASHINGTON DC//J7-JEDD//

b. Routine changes should be submitted electronically to the Deputy Director, Joint and Coalition Warfighting, Joint Doctrine Support Division and info the lead agent and the Director for Joint Force Development, J-7/JEDD.

c. When a Joint Staff directorate submits a proposal to the CJCS that would change source document information reflected in this publication, that directorate will include a proposed change to this publication as an enclosure to its proposal. The Services and other organizations are requested to notify the Joint Staff J-7 when changes to source documents reflected in this publication are initiated.

5. Distribution of Publications

Local reproduction is authorized and access to unclassified publications is unrestricted. However, access to and reproduction authorization for classified JPs must be in accordance with DOD Manual 5200.1, *Information Security Program: Overview, Classification, and Declassification.*

6. Distribution of Electronic Publications

a. Joint Staff J-7 will not print copies of JPs for distribution. Electronic versions are available on JDEIS at https://jdeis.js.mil (NIPRNET) and http://jdeis.js.smil.mil (SIPRNET), and on the JEL at http://www.dtic.mil/doctrine (NIPRNET).

b. Only approved JPs and joint test publications are releasable outside the CCMDs, Services, and Joint Staff. Release of any classified JP to foreign governments or foreign nationals must be requested through the local embassy (Defense Attaché Office) to DIA, Defense Foreign Liaison/IE-3, 200 MacDill Blvd., Joint Base Anacostia-Bolling, Washington, DC 20340-5100.

c. JEL CD-ROM. Upon request of a joint doctrine development community member, the Joint Staff J-7 will produce and deliver one CD-ROM with current JPs. This JEL CD-ROM will be updated not less than semiannually and when received can be locally reproduced for use within the CCMDs and Services.

GLOSSARY
PART I—ABBREVIATIONS AND ACRONYMS

AJP	allied joint publication
AOR	area of responsibility
C2	command and control
CCDR	combatant commander
CCIR	commander's critical information requirement
CCMD	combatant command
CJCS	Chairman of the Joint Chiefs of Staff
CJCSI	Chairman of the Joint Chiefs of Staff instruction
CJCSM	Chairman of the Joint Chiefs of Staff manual
CMO	civil-military operations
CO	cyberspace operations
COA	course of action
CONOPS	concept of operations
CONPLAN	concept plan
DOD	Department of Defense
DODD	Department of Defense directive
DODI	Department of Defense instruction
EEI	essential element of information
EMS	electromagnetic spectrum
EW	electronic warfare
EWC	electronic warfare cell
FDO	flexible deterrent option
GCC	geographic combatant commander
IA	information assurance
IO	information operations
IOCB	information operations coordination board
IOII	information operations intelligence integration
IRC	information-related capability
J-2	intelligence directorate of a joint staff
J-3	operations directorate of a joint staff
J-39 DDGO	Joint Staff, Deputy Director for Global Operations
JCEWS	joint force commander's electronic warfare staff
JEMSO	joint electromagnetic spectrum operations
JFC	joint force commander
JIACG	joint interagency coordination group
JIOWC	Joint Information Operations Warfare Center

JIPOE	joint intelligence preparation of the operational environment
JISE	joint intelligence support element
JOPG	joint operations planning group
JOPP	joint operation planning process
JP	joint publication
JPG	joint planning group
JTCB	joint targeting coordination board
KLE	key leader engagement
MILDEC	military deception
MISO	military information support operations
MNF	multinational force
MNFC	multinational force commander
MOE	measure of effectiveness
MOEI	measure of effectiveness indicator
MOP	measure of performance
NDP	national disclosure policy
OPLAN	operation plan
OPORD	operation order
OPSEC	operations security
PA	public affairs
PIR	priority intelligence requirement
RFI	request for information
ROE	rules of engagement
SC	strategic communication
STO	special technical operations
TA	target audience
TCP	theater campaign plan
USC	United States Code
USD(I)	Under Secretary of Defense for Intelligence
USD(P)	Under Secretary of Defense for Policy
USG	United States Government
USSTRATCOM	United States Strategic Command

PART II—TERMS AND DEFINITIONS

computer network attack. None. (Approved for removal from JP 1-02.)

computer network defense. None. (Approved for removal from JP 1-02.)

computer network exploitation. None. (Approved for removal from JP 1-02.)

computer network operations. None. (Approved for removal from JP 1-02.)

data. None. (Approved for removal from JP 1-02.)

data item. None. (Approved for removal from JP 1-02.)

defense information infrastructure. None. (Approved for removal from JP 1-02.)

defense support to public diplomacy. None. (Approved for removal from JP 1-02.)

global information infrastructure. None. (Approved for removal from JP 1-02.)

information-based processes. None. (Approved for removal from JP 1-02.)

information environment. The aggregate of individuals, organizations, and systems that collect, process, disseminate, or act on information. (JP 1-02. SOURCE: JP 3-13)

information operations. The integrated employment, during military operations, of information-related capabilities in concert with other lines of operation to influence, disrupt, corrupt, or usurp the decision-making of adversaries and potential adversaries while protecting our own. Also called **IO.** (Approved for incorporation into JP 1-02 with JP 3-13 as the source JP.)

information operations intelligence integration. The integration of intelligence disciplines and analytic methods to characterize and forecast, identify vulnerabilities, determine effects, and assess the information environment. Also called **IOII.** (Approved for inclusion in JP 1-02.)

information-related capability. A tool, technique, or activity employed within a dimension of the information environment that can be used to create effects and operationally desirable conditions. Also called **IRC.** (Approved for inclusion in JP 1-02.)

information security. None. (Approved for removal from JP 1-02.)

information superiority. The operational advantage derived from the ability to collect, process, and disseminate an uninterrupted flow of information while exploiting or denying an adversary's ability to do the same. (JP 1-02. SOURCE: JP 3-13)

information system. None. (Approved for removal from JP 1-02.)

national information infrastructure. None. (Approved for removal from JP 1-02.)

probe. None. (Approved for removal from JP 1-02.)

special information operations. None. (Approved for removal from JP 1-02.)

target audience. An individual or group selected for influence. Also called **TA.** (JP 1-02. SOURCE: JP 3-13)

JOINT DOCTRINE PUBLICATIONS HIERARCHY

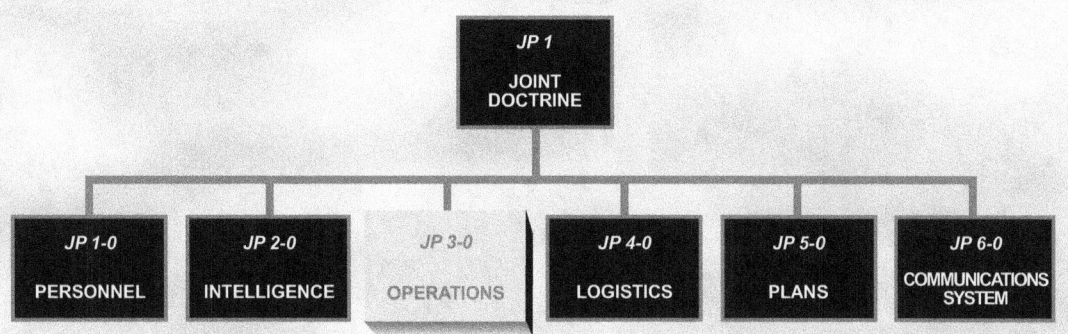

All joint publications are organized into a comprehensive hierarchy as shown in the chart above. **Joint Publication (JP) 3-13** is in the **Operations** series of joint doctrine publications. The diagram below illustrates an overview of the development process:

STEP #4 - Maintenance

- JP published and continuously assessed by users
- Formal assessment begins 24 27 months following publication
- Revision begins 3.5 years after publication
- Each JP revision is completed no later than 5 years after signature

STEP #1 - Initiation

- Joint doctrine development community (JDDC) submission to fill extant operational void
- Joint Staff (JS) J 7 conducts front end analysis
- Joint Doctrine Planning Conference validation
- Program directive (PD) development and staffing/joint working group
- PD includes scope, references, outline, milestones, and draft authorship
- JS J 7 approves and releases PD to lead agent (LA) (Service, combatant command, JS directorate)

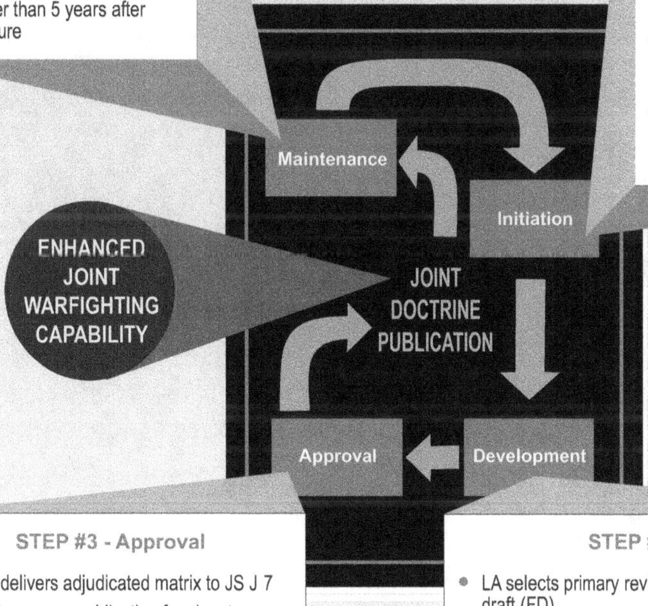

Maintenance

Initiation

ENHANCED JOINT WARFIGHTING CAPABILITY

JOINT DOCTRINE PUBLICATION

Approval

Development

STEP #3 - Approval

- JSDS delivers adjudicated matrix to JS J 7
- JS J 7 prepares publication for signature
- JSDS prepares JS staffing package
- JSDS staffs the publication via JSAP for signature

STEP #2 - Development

- LA selects primary review authority (PRA) to develop the first draft (FD)
- PRA develops FD for staffing with JDDC
- FD comment matrix adjudication
- JS J 7 produces the final coordination (FC) draft, staffs to JDDC and JS via Joint Staff Action Processing (JSAP) system
- Joint Staff doctrine sponsor (JSDS) adjudicates FC comment matrix
- FC joint working group